Checklist *for* My Family

A Guide to My History, Financial Plans, and Final Wishes

SECOND EDITION

Sally Balch Hurme

ABA AMERICAN BAR ASSOCIATION

AARP

Cover design by Jill Tedhams/ABA Design

Printed in the United States of America.

26 25 24 23 22   5 4 3 2 1

A catalog record for this book is available from the Library of Congress.

Discounts are available for books ordered in bulk. Special consideration is given to state bars, CLE programs, and other bar-related organizations. Inquire at Book Publishing, ABA Publishing, American Bar Association, 321 N. Clark Street, Chicago, Illinois 60654-7598.

www.shopABA.org

CONTENTS AT A GLANCE

TABLE OF CONTENTS

INTRODUCTION
A GIFT TO YOURSELF AND YOUR FAMILY

For years, I put off getting organized: Putting those bills on autopay. Labeling those photos sitting in boxes on my bedroom floor. Keeping track of all my passwords. Updating my will.

But it weighed on me. It wasn't just that the mess made me crazy—that I couldn't find that password, that I couldn't recall who had prescribed that medication for my husband. It was also my concern that, should something happen to me, I was leaving my family in the dark. Yet I didn't know how to get started.

If you're reading this book, there's a good chance that you, too, are ready to get your life in order and make sure your family knows your plans and wishes. That's where I step in: to set out what you need to do, to simplify the process, and to nudge you each step of the way.

In the following pages, I guide you through the process of gathering in one place your financial information, legal documents, online accounts, wishes about medical care, and much more. Plus, I tell you what you need, why you need it, and where to get it, if it is missing.

While giving you peace of mind, this book is also a gift to your family. I've known too many families who were thrown into turmoil when a loved one started to develop signs of dementia or suddenly became ill. Relatives needed to know where the Social Security benefits were deposited, whether life insurance premiums were paid, and when utility bills were automatically paid, but no one knew the location of the accounts or the passwords. They scrambled to find information about their loved one's medical insurance and current medications. By assembling the information in these checklists, you can gift to your family members the confidence that they are doing the right things.

In This Book

The chapters are arranged for you to set out your history, assets and liabilities, legal documents, and medical and final wishes.

In Chapter 1, you can provide your personal history. Perhaps even more important to you and to your family than your investments and lists of passwords is the cherished legacy you can provide by passing on your recollections about your own life, interests, accomplishments, and other special remembrances. Chapter 1 also includes one of the most important checklists in this book: Where You Can Find It, a ready reference to what you have and where you've put it. In Chapter 2, you can outline your family history, sharing your memories and knowledge of those who came before you.

In Chapters 3 through 9, you can detail your assets and liabilities to help clarify your financial status and make plans with that in mind. This clarity will also ease the process of handling your estate and make your family members aware of the resources they may be entitled to. You'll document your insurance in Chapter 3; your banking and savings in Chapter 4; and your investments, including your retirement accounts, in Chapters 5 and 6. I walk you through benefits such as Medicare and Social Security, and ask you to gather the information necessary for your family to apply for any survivor benefits they would be eligible to receive upon your death. Chapter 7 is devoted to veterans, listing and explaining the wide array of benefits available to those of you who have served our country. Chapter 8 walks you through any real estate you may own, and Chapter 9 makes manageable your other personal assets—including digital assets, jewelry, artwork, and any storage units you may rent—that has value to you and your family.

In Chapter 10, you can review the legal documents that you and your family need and note where they are located. For those of you who may not have gotten started on this aspect, not to worry. I offer a primer so you can begin.

In Chapter 11, you can set out what you would like your family to do should you become ill or upon your death. I've known people who live together for decades without discussing their wishes regarding life support, organ donations, funeral or memorial services, and burial or cremation. Without meaning to do so, we can leave many distressing decisions for our loved ones. You can make it so much easier on your family by simply deciding on and putting in writing what you want and expect. The more decisions you make, the fewer decisions your family must make in a time of emotional turmoil.

This book should bring both you and your family members comfort and peace of mind. They won't have to be scrambling to find documents or guessing what you might have wanted them to do. Filling out these checklists will make everyone's life easier.

How to Use This Book

Each chapter starts with a ***to-do checklist*** you can use as you collect the information you want to gather. Then I walk you through the to-do items that might need explaining, with basic information about each, why it is important, how to locate it, and ways to organize it.

After the explanations, you'll find ***action checklists*** where you provide a detailed record of the topic that chapter covers, such as your personal history, family history, financial assets, medical records, and final wishes.

Don't expect to complete this guide in one or two sittings. You may need to spend time digging through old records or random drawers and contemplating how you'd like to handle things. I'm still working on organizing old photographs and slides, a seemingly never-ending job because I keep finding more stashed in strange places.

But don't look upon completing this book as a task. If you approach each chapter in manageable chunks and view it as a fascinating family project, a way to simplify your life, and a gift to yourself and those you love, you will find great satisfaction in tracking down bits and pieces of your family history, locating the missing birth certificates, and shredding unnecessary papers.

Here are ten quick tips to make this project manageable:

1. Choose your method for completing the checklists. I've provided two options:
   a) This book is for you to write in. You can fill in the paper checklists with a pencil or erasable pen. If your decisions or assets change as time goes by, just erase and update. You'll need to write legibly. After all, if you take the time to create this record, you'll want to be able to read it—and have your family be able to read it. If your handwriting is awful, like mine, you'll probably want to go with the next option.
   b) You can download the checklists in this book from the ABA website at **ambar.org/AARPforms**. I provide both Word and fillable PDF formats to choose from. The digital downloads make it easy to fill out the checklists on your computer and to make changes so that they are up to date.
2. Scan through the list of to-do checklists at the beginning of each chapter to get an overview of the range of topics it covers.
3. Scratch off the items that don't apply to your circumstances. It will be satisfying to see how much you've already taken care of or don't need to bother with.
4. Modify the checklists. Not every item on every checklist will apply to you. The electronic forms make it especially easy for you to make modifications. You can, for example, delete sections that don't apply or add more lines or sections. But even if you use the book pages, you can tailor the checklists to your unique needs.
5. Tackle the easy parts first. You may find that you want to start with just one section or checklist that is the easiest for you to accomplish.
6. Check off each item on the to-do checklists as you complete that step. That said, don't rush. Take the time you need to answer the questions and collect the information. You'll find clues in the chapters.
7. Prioritize. What should be completed sooner rather than later? Your priority list is unique to you. For my husband and me, I put at the top of my list writing down our medical wishes through advance directives (see Chapter 11), recording our

medications (see Chapter 1), and talking with our lawyer about how we wanted our property distributed upon our death (see Chapter 10). My second-level priorities were planning our funerals (see Chapter 11) and getting our important papers in one place and noting where to find them (see Chapter 1).

8. Store the completed checklists in a binder or computer folder. As you complete a chapter, you may want to photocopy the book pages or print out a copy of the checklists and place the pages in a three-ring binder. Or you may choose to keep the electronic checklists in a folder on your computer. If you're storing pages in a binder, you may also want to add plastic sleeves to slip in clippings or documents that you want to save. For example, you may want to add your original homeowners insurance policy. If you're saving electronically, you could scan the document and add the file to your checklist folder. Be sure to note on the Where to Find It checklist in Chapter 1 where you have stored or saved those documents so they will be readily available.
9. Keep the checklists up to date. Whichever system you use, revise the checklists as changes occur. Review the checklists at least once a year. Set aside a few hours to update the forms and add new information. Just after you have pulled together records to prepare your taxes is a good time to review and update your checklists.
10. Discuss this book with your family members. Let them know that you have taken the time to gather the valuable information in this book and tell them where your checklists are located and what your wishes are. Your family needs to know how to locate this treasure trove of information. With it, your loved ones can carry out your plans and wishes. Whether it is how you want your personal things distributed among your family and friends, what sort of medical care you desire, or how you wish to be buried, make sure at least one trusted person knows what you want.

A word of caution: You are assembling a great deal of very personal information that, in the wrong hands, could be used to your disadvantage. Unfortunately, there are unscrupulous people who do not have your best interests in mind. They may even be people you think you should be able to trust. While they may not admit it, some relatives may be more concerned about their own interests than yours. In some families, it is difficult or even impossible to reach a consensus or agreement on just about anything. Be cautious about whom you share the information with. The nosy neighbor, the distant relative, or the casual friend may not be able to keep confidential this very private information.

A word of encouragement: These records can be of significant interest and value to you during your lifetime and can provide a sense of personal freedom. I've heard from many readers of the first edition of this book that now that they have the information organized, they frequently and easily refer to the checklists for information they need. And they trust that their family will have the information it needs to follow their wishes and handle their affairs.

CHAPTER 1
MY PERSONAL HISTORY

No one knows your personal history as well as you do. Chances are good that your children, family, and significant others may not know as much about you as you might think. But it's some of the most valuable information you hold, so it's an important—and fun—place to start your journey.

While making sure the information passed on to later generations is accurate, you can enjoy tracking down bits of information and remembering key events in your life, such as all the places you've lived, the different work experiences you've had, and the hobbies and activities you've enjoyed through the years.

Haven't you wondered about similar details surrounding your parents or grandparents? Most of us become more interested in family history as we grow older, but unless someone records that history for us, it will be lost. *You* are the one who can best gather this for your family.

The checklists in this chapter provide places to enter detailed information about you—your educational background, where you have lived and worked, organizations you have belonged to, awards you have received, and information about your pets, religious or political activities, and hobbies. I had fun recalling the names of my childhood pets—Fluffy, Blackie, Bostwick, Sandy, and Hale—and even found photos of each of them. Worried about where you'll find some of the more important information? I also offer useful tips for tracking it down.

The Contacts checklist should be easier to collect. It's a record of the people you regularly interact with and rely on and with whom your family may need to get in touch. You'll want to include their contact information and update the list frequently.

The Where to Find It checklist may be the most important checklist in this book to help you get and stay organized. Once you have identified that you have an item, where is it now? Where *have* you put the keys to your safe deposit box and the combination for the lock on your extra storage shed? You never know when you or your family will need to find a copy of your contract for your security system or your homeowners insurance policy. (In subsequent chapters, you can record other details about these various documents.)

Don't overlook the Medication Record, where you'll list all your prescriptions and over-the-counter medications and supplements. Carry a copy of this page with you in your wallet or scan it into your phone in case of emergency and to review current medications with your medical professionals.

Finally, you will find a page entitled "Other." This is for you to fill in with personal notes about yourself—your interests, accomplishments, thoughts, or desires. Add anything you consider to be of interest to your family. Don't be modest! If you did something in your lifetime you're proud of, jot it down. Loved ones will be proud, too. If something very humorous happened to you, they will enjoy it. Remember how you were fascinated with the interesting stories your parents and grandparents told you? Your family members are just as interested in your remembrances.

At the time of your death, some of the information you record in these checklists can be used in the preparation of a death certificate, obituary, income tax returns, and many other documents, as well as what your family will need when applying for survivors benefits.

My To-Do Checklist

Done	Need to Do	
❑	❑	Get copies of your birth certificate and marriage licenses
❑	❑	Get copies of citizenship/naturalization documents
❑	❑	Get copies of divorce decrees
❑	❑	Record the medications you take
❑	❑	Organize tax files by year
❑	❑	List all employers
❑	❑	Keep safe original documents that are valuable or irreplaceable
❑	❑	Complete the checklists for Chapter 1

✔ Get certified copies of your birth certificate and marriage licenses

The first item on your to-do list is to get two certified copies of your birth certificate and marriage licenses if you don't already hold them in your possession. You may need these documents to apply for your passport, renew your driver license, or apply for public benefits for you or your family, and your family will need them to settle your estate and apply for various survivor benefits. To be a "certified copy," it must have a statement by an official that it is a true copy of an original.

If you can't put your hands on these important documents, start the process now to obtain copies. While you are tracking down your papers, why not obtain copies for the rest of your immediate family members? That way they'll have those records when needed.

Where can you find them? Most births and marriages are reported to the proper local authorities to maintain a lasting record. Each state has its own method of maintaining these records. Birth certificates and marriage licenses can usually be obtained from the clerk, registrar, or recorder of the county in which the birth or marriage took place.

To find your documents, go to www.cdc.gov/nchs/w2w.htm, a website maintained by the Centers for Disease Control and Prevention (CDC) that lists, for each state, where to write or call to obtain these records and often the cost per certificate.

Fees generally range from $2 to $20 for each certified copy. Additional copies may be available at reduced rates. Some states may request that you enclose a self-addressed, stamped envelope for the return of your documents. Other states have a website where some records can be downloaded electronically.

Many states will not issue copies of birth certificates or marriage licenses unless the requestor is closely related to the person named in the certificate. Therefore, when requesting records for someone else in your family, it is important to identify yourself as the spouse, parent, or child.

Once you have the documents, store them in a safe deposit box. And, finally, record their location in the Where to Find It checklist in this chapter. There are rare instances in which you won't be able to obtain these documents. For example, in the not-too-distant past, many births occurred in private homes and went unrecorded. Occasionally, fire destroys courthouses or other record depositories. Records may be incorrect because of misspelling, changes in spelling, illegible handwriting, misunderstanding of names, and other errors. If you can't obtain them, note that, too, on the Where to Find It checklist.

✔ Get copies of citizenship/naturalization documents

Proof of citizenship or immigration status can be vitally important when you or your family member is applying for many benefits. If you have lost or can't find your citizenship/naturalization documents, you can request replacement copies from the U.S. Citizenship and Immigration Services. You'll need form N-565, which you can download at www.uscis.gov/n-565. That site also provides instructions on where to file the form and how to sign up for an electronic account to receive future alerts and status updates.

✔ Get copies of divorce decrees

Your family will also need certified copies of judgments of divorce or annulment to apply for Social Security death or survivor benefits, veterans benefits, and private pension plan disbursements. You obtain them from the clerk or registrar of the court that granted the divorce or annulment. Once again, the fee for obtaining copies varies in each state and may also depend upon the number of pages in the document.

Call or write a letter to the clerk of the court that granted the decree or judgment to inquire about the cost of obtaining a copy of the document. When requesting copies, you'll need to give the names of the spouses, case number (if you know it), type of divorce, and date and place the divorce or annulment was granted. Enclose a self-addressed, stamped envelope along with your payment of any fee and a phone number where you can be reached in case of questions.

✔ Complete a Medication Record

Carrying with you at all times a record of current medications can be lifesaving. If you should have a sudden illness or be in an accident, emergency responders and your family need to know promptly what medications you have been taking, the medical conditions for which you are receiving treatment, and any drug allergies you might have.

On the Medication Record in this chapter, list your prescription drugs as well as any over-the-counter drugs, vitamins, and herbal and dietary supplements. Include the reason you are taking each medication, prescribing physician, and pharmacy. If you are not sure why you are taking a prescribed medication, ask your doctor. You can also list whether the medication is a pill, liquid, patch, or injection, and what dosage you take: how many milligrams are in each tablet. Note the frequency, too, such as "one pill at breakfast" in the "When/How Taken" column, along with any special directions, such as "with food."

Carry a copy with you all the time and share this information with your pharmacists and medical professionals. At each appointment, review the list with your doctors. Every time I go to the doctor, I'm glad I have my handy list of medications to make sure that every doctor knows all the medications I am taking and that my medication records are accurate. Also make sure that a family member keeps a copy of the list, and, if you have caregivers, ask them to carry a copy, too. I keep an extra copy of my medication list on my refrigerator door where first responders can easily find it.

✔ Organize tax files by year

Having your tax returns organized is an immediate benefit to you. Chances are good that when you apply for a loan, the lender will want to have copies of the last two years' returns. You'll know quickly where to go to get those copies. An added benefit: Having these documents in one place helps you prepare your next year's tax return.

Your past tax returns can also be an invaluable source of information for your executor or administrator of your estate (your personal representative). Your personal representative will be responsible for filing your income tax return for the year of your death and possibly estate state and federal tax returns. Being able to readily locate recent returns and the supporting documentation for any schedules or itemized deductions will save your executor much time and frustration.

I keep each year's return and all the supporting documents in a portable file box, with separate folders for donations, deductions, mortgage statements, and W-2 and 1099 forms. I store each file box for seven years on a high shelf in my basement. After seven years, I go through and shred the supporting documentation that is no longer essential to keep for any IRS auditing purposes. I then use that emptied box for the upcoming year's collection of documents. I've saved every year's tax return going all the way back to my first return if for no other reason than they are historical recollections of how times have changed.

If you file your return electronically, be certain to keep an electronic file of the return in a clearly labeled folder in your computer along with scans of the necessary supporting documentation. I name my folder "[Year] Tax Return Docs."

✔ List all employers

Listing your past employers can help you track down any benefits you are entitled to now. Besides, it is fun to remember and record those first jobs as a camp counselor, lifeguard, grocery bagger, or car hop. And by listing all your past employers, your executor will be able to quickly identify places to check for any benefits, pensions, retirement accounts, insurance benefits, or even unpaid leave that might be available for your heirs.

✔ Keep safe original documents that are valuable or irreplaceable

You don't want to turn finding papers into a scavenger hunt for you or your family. Use the Where to Find It checklist starting on page 37 to record where you keep many of your records, lists, and documents, including copies or files of all the checklists in this book. It may be a safe deposit box for the most important documents—not what you need to update frequently or readily access. You'll find more information about safe deposit boxes in Chapter 4. Or it may be in a desk drawer, fireproof box in the den, filing cabinet in the basement, or a computer file.

It's important to let your family know where you have placed these items for safe keeping. If you are not sure where something is located, now might be a good time to locate it. If you don't know where it is, your family may have an even harder time finding it.

PERSONAL HISTORY ACTION CHECKLISTS

The checklists in Chapter 1 are set out in the following order:

- *Basic Personal Information*
- *Biography*
- *Contacts*
- *Health and Medication Record*
- *Awards and Accomplishments*
- *Education*
- *Employment*
- *Memberships*
- *Pets*
- *Religion, Politics, and Hobbies*
- *Residences*
- *Where to Find It*
- *Personal History: Other Highlights*

You can download these checklists in Word or fillable PDF format at **ambar.org/AARPforms**.

Basic Personal Information

Name: ____
First *Middle* *Last*

Name at birth, if different: ______________________________
First *Middle* *Last*

Place of birth: ______________________________________
City *State* *Country*

Date of birth: ______________________________________

Date of adoption: ____________________________________

Legal name change: __________________________________
First *Middle* *Last*

Date of legal name change: ____________________________

Legal name change court: ______________________________
County *City* *State*

****

Current address: _____________________________________

Number of years: ____________________________________

Home phone: ____________________ Cell phone: ____________________

E-mail: ____________________ Fax: ____________________

****

Citizenship: ____

- ❑ By birth
- ❑ By naturalization

Naturalization date: ______________________________

Naturalization place: ______________________________
County *City* *State*

****

Military veteran:

- ❑ Yes
- ❑ No

Branch of service: ______________________________

Dates of service: ______________________________

Serial # (DD214): ______________ Rank: ______________

Type of discharge: ______________________________

****

Social Security #: ______________________________

Passport #: ______________________ Expiration: __________

Country of issue: ______________________________

Driver's license or state ID card #: ______________ Expiration: __________

State of issue: ______________________________

****

Voter registration:

Precinct: __________ County: ______________ State: __________

****

Faith/Denomination: ______________________________

Place of worship: ______________________________

Address: ______________________________

Pastor/Priest/Rabbi/Spiritual leader: ______________________________

Phone: ______________ E-mail: ______________________

****

Blood type: ______________________________

****

Marital status:

- ❑ Divorced
- ❑ Married
- ❑ Never married
- ❑ Widowed

First Spouse

Name: ______________________________

Phone: ______________ E-mail: ______________________

Address: ______________________________

Name of spouse at birth (if different): ______________________________

Date of birth: ______________________________

Place of birth: ______________________________

Date of marriage: ______________________________

Date of divorce: ______________________________

Date of death: ______________________________

Place of burial: ______________________________

Cause of death: ______________________________

Second Spouse

Name: ______________________________

Phone: ______________ E-mail: ______________

Address: ______________________________

Name of spouse at birth (if different): ______________________________

Date of birth: ______________________________

Place of birth: ______________________________

Date of marriage: ______________________________

Date of divorce: ______________________________

Date of death: ______________________________

Place of burial: ______________________________

Cause of death: ______________________________

Biography

Highlights of my life:

Contacts

Advisers

Accountant: ____________________

Phone: ____________ E-mail: ____________

Website: ____________________

Address: ____________________

Attorney: ____________________

Phone: ____________ E-mail: ____________

Website: ____________________

Address: ____________________

Banker: ____________________

Phone: ____________ E-mail: ____________

Website: ____________________

Address: ____________________

Executor: ____________________

Phone: ____________ E-mail: ____________

Website: ____________________

Address: ____________________

Insurance agent: ____

Phone: ______________________ E-mail: ______________________________

Website: ____

Address: ____

Investment adviser: ____

Phone: ______________________ E-mail: ______________________________

Website: ____

Address: ____

Tax adviser: ____

Phone: ______________________ E-mail: ______________________________

Website: ____

Address: ____

Spiritual leader/Pastor/Priest/Rabbi: ________________________________

Phone: ______________________ E-mail: ______________________________

Website: ____

Address: ____

Other: ______________________________

Phone: ____________________ E-mail: ____________________

Website: ______________________________

Address: ______________________________

Medical Professionals

Primary physician: ______________________________

Phone: ____________________ E-mail: ____________________

Website: ______________________________

Address: ______________________________

Specialty physician: ______________________________

Phone: ____________________ E-mail: ____________________

Website: ______________________________

Address: ______________________________

Specialty physician: ______________________________

Phone: ____________________ E-mail: ____________________

Website: ______________________________

Address: ______________________________

Specialty physician: ______________________________

Phone: ______________ E-mail: ______________

Website: ______________________________

Address: ______________________________

Dentist: ______________________________

Phone: ______________ E-mail: ______________

Website: ______________________________

Address: ______________________________

Other: ______________________________

Phone: ______________ E-mail: ______________

Website: ______________________________

Address: ______________________________

Service Providers

Housekeeper: ______________________________

Phone: ______________ E-mail: ______________

Website: ______________________________

Address: ______________________________

Lawn service/Gardener: ______________________________

Phone: ____________________ E-mail: ____________________

Website: ______________________________

Address: ______________________________

Home health agency: ______________________________

Phone: ____________________ E-mail: ____________________

Website: ______________________________

Address: ______________________________

Home maintenance: ______________________________

Phone: ____________________ E-mail: ____________________

Website: ______________________________

Address: ______________________________

Property manager: ______________________________

Phone: ____________________ E-mail: ____________________

Website: ______________________________

Address: ______________________________

Security system: ____

Phone: ____________________ E-mail: ______________________________

Website:____

Address: ____

Veterinarian: ____

Phone: ____________________ E-mail: ______________________________

Website:____

Address: ____

Health and Medication Record

My Personal Information:

Name: ______________________________

Date of birth: ______________________________

Phone: ______________________________

Emergency Contact:

Name: ______________________________

Relationship: ______________________________

Phone : ______________________________

Primary Care Physician:

Name: ______________________________

Phone: ______________________________

Website: ______________________________

Pharmacies:

Name: ______________________________

Phone: ______________________________

Website: ______________________________

Name: ______________________________

Phone: ______________________________

Website: ______________________________

Other Health Care Providers:

Name: ______________________________

Specialty: ______________________________

Phone: ______________________________

Website: ______________________________

Name: ______________________________

Specialty: ______________________________

Phone: ______________________________

Website: ______________________________

My Medical Conditions:

____

____

____

____

____

____

____

____

My Allergies:

My Health Notes:

Medications

Medication	Reason	Dosage and Form (Pill, Liquid, Patch, Injection)	When/How Taken	Prescriber and Contact Info	Pharmacy and Contact Info

Be sure to include *all* prescription drugs, over-the-counter drugs, vitamins, and herbal or dietary supplements.

Awards and Accomplishments

Academic awards and accomplishments:

Athletic awards and accomplishments:

Work-related awards and commendations:

Education

Elementary schools:

Name of school: ______________________________

Location: ______________________________

Grades attended: ____________ Dates attended: ______________________

Name of school: ______________________________

Location: ______________________________

Grades attended: ____________ Dates attended: ______________________

Middle or junior high schools:

Name of school: ______________________________

Location: ______________________________

Grades attended: ____________ Dates attended: ______________________

Name of school: ______________________________

Location: ______________________________

Grades attended: ____________ Dates attended: ______________________

High schools:

Name of school: ______________________________

Location: ______________________________

Grades attended: ____________ Dates attended: ______________________

Name of school: ______________________________

Location: ______________________________

Grades attended: ____________ Dates attended: ______________________

Colleges or universities:

Name of school: ____________________

Location: ____________________

Degree/Certificate: ____________________

Dates attended/Graduated: ____________________

Name of school: ____________________

Location: ____________________

Degree/Certificate: ____________________

Dates attended/Graduated: ____________________

Additional schools and training programs:

Name of school: ____________________

Location: ____________________

Degree/Certificate: ____________________

Dates attended/Graduated: ____________________

Name of school: ____________________

Location: ____________________

Degree/Certificate: ____________________

Dates attended/Graduated: ____________________

Extracurricular activities (art, athletics, debate, drama, fraternity or sorority, music, school newspaper, etc.):

Employment

Current employment:

Employer: ____________________

Address: ____________________

Contact: ____________________

Type of work/Job title: ____________________

Previous employment:

Employer: ____________________

Address: ____________________

Contact: ____________________

Type of work/Job title: ____________________

Dates: ____________________

Employer: ____________________

Address: ____________________

Contact: ____________________

Type of work/Job title: ____________________

Dates: ____________________

Employer: ______________________________

Address: ______________________________

Contact: ______________________________

Type of work/Job title: ______________________________

Dates: ______________________________

Employer: ______________________________

Address: ______________________________

Contact: ______________________________

Type of work/Job title: ______________________________

Dates: ______________________________

Employer: ______________________________

Address: ______________________________

Contact: ______________________________

Type of work/Job title: ______________________________

Dates: ______________________________

Employer: ______________________________

Address: ______________________________

Contact: ______________________________

Type of work/Job title: ______________________________

Dates: ______________________________

Date of retirement: ______________________________

Work accomplishments and interesting projects:

____

____

____

____

____

____

____

____

____

____

____

____

____

____

Memberships

Membership organization: ______________________________

Website:______________________________

Address: ______________________________

Involvement: ______________________________

Dates of membership: ______________________________

Interesting facts: ______________________________

Membership organization: ______________________________

Website:______________________________

Address: ______________________________

Involvement: ______________________________

Interesting facts: ______________________________

Dates of membership: ______________________________

Membership organization: ______________________________

Website:______________________________

Address: ______________________________

Involvement: ______________________________

Interesting facts: ______________________________

Dates of membership: ______________________________

Membership organization: ______________________________

Website: ______________________________

Address: ______________________________

Involvement: ______________________________

Interesting facts: ______________________________

Dates of membership: ______________________________

I have the following season tickets:

Sports: ______________________________

Website: ______________________________

Address: ______________________________

Seat numbers: ______________________________

Theater: ______________________________

Website: ______________________________

Address: ______________________________

Seat numbers: ______________________________

Pets

Pet name: ____________________ Type/Species/Coloring: ________________________

Birth date: ____________________ Ownership/Adoption date: ____________________

Instructions on food, water, care, exercise, medication, conditions: ___________________

____

____

Veterinarian: ____

Phone: ______________________ Website:_______________________________________

Address: ____

E-mail: ____

Breeder:____

Phone: ______________________ Website:_______________________________________

Address: ____

E-mail: ____

Groomer:____

Phone: ______________________ Website:_______________________________________

Address: ____

E-mail: ____

Pet name: ____________________ Type/Species/Coloring: ________________________

Birth date: ____________________ Ownership/Adoption date: __________________

Instructions on food, water, care, exercise, medication, conditions: ________________

____

____

Veterinarian: ____

Phone: ______________________ Website:_______________________________________

Address: ____

E-mail: ____

Breeder:____

Phone: ______________________ Website:_______________________________________

Address: ____

E-mail: ____

Groomer:____

Phone: ______________________ Website:_______________________________________

Address: ____

E-mail: ____

(See Chapter 11 on page 263 describing my wishes for the further care of my pets.)

Religion, Politics, and Hobbies

My religious activities and beliefs:

My politics:

My hobbies:

Residences

Current and former homes:

Address: ____

City: ______________________ State: _____ Dates: __________________

Address: ____

City: ______________________ State: _____ Dates: __________________

Address: ____

City: ______________________ State: _____ Dates: __________________

Address: ____

City: ______________________ State: _____ Dates: __________________

Address: ____

City: ______________________ State: _____ Dates: __________________

Address: ____

City: ______________________ State: _____ Dates: __________________

Address: ____

City: ______________________ State: _____ Dates: __________________

Address: ____

City: ______________________ State: _____ Dates: __________________

Address: ____

City: ____________________ State: ______ Dates: ________________

Address: ____

City: ____________________ State: ______ Dates: ________________

Address: ____

City: ____________________ State: ______ Dates: ________________

Address: ____

City: ____________________ State: ______ Dates: ________________

Address: ____

City: ____________________ State: ______ Dates: ________________

Address: ____

City: ____________________ State: ______ Dates: ________________

Address: ____

City: ____________________ State: ______ Dates: ________________

Address: ____

City: ____________________ State: ______ Dates: ________________

Address: ____

City: ____________________ State: ______ Dates: ________________

Where to Find It

Where to find my safe deposit box:

Bank name: ______________________________

Address: ______________________________

Box number: ______________________________

Personal and Family Records	Where to Find It
Adoption papers	
Alimony settlement agreement	
Annulment decrees or judgments	
Appointment book or calendar	
Award certificates	
Birth certificates	
Caregiving information: Children	
Caregiving information: Parents	
Change of name certificates	
Citizenship/naturalization papers	
Civic awards	
Cohabitation agreement	
Digital photos	
Divorce decrees or judgments	
Driver's license	
Educational diplomas and certificates	

Personal and Family Records	Where to Find It
Educational transcripts	
Family tree	
Keys to post office box	
Keys to residence	
Keys to other real estate	
Keys to safe deposit box	
Keys to storage unit	
Keys to vehicles	
Lock combinations	
Marriage licenses	
Membership certificates	
Military awards	
Military separation papers	
Music/CDs catalog	
Passport	
Passwords	
Pet adoption papers	
Pet care instructions	
Pet trust	
Photos and photo albums	
Power of attorney for health care	

Personal and Family Records	Where to Find It
Power of attorney for finances	
Postnuptial agreement	
Prenuptial agreement	
Property settlement agreement	
Qualified Domestic Relations Order (QDRO)	
Security system information	
Storage unit contract	
Tax returns and records	
Other	
Other	

Insurance Records	Where to Find It
Annuities	
Boat insurance	
Dental insurance card	
Drug plan card	
Homeowners insurance	
Life insurance	
Long-term care insurance	
Medical insurance	

Insurance Records	Where to Find It
Medicare card	
Medicare Advantage plan	
Medicare Part D card	
Medicare supplemental plan	
Medicare summary notices	
Pre-need funeral contract	
Renters insurance	
Umbrella insurance	
Vehicle insurance	
Other	
Other	
Other	
Other	

Benefit and Investment Records	Where to Find It
401(k) agreements	
403(b) agreements	
Bearer Bonds	
Bitcoin	
Brokerage account statements	
Certificates of deposit	

Benefit and Investment Records	Where to Find It
Checking account statements	
Credit union account statements	
IRA agreements/statements	
Military separation papers	
Pension agreements	
Savings account statements	
Savings bonds	
SEP agreements/statements	
Social Security benefit statement	
Social Security card	
Workers' compensation documentation	
Other	
Other	
Other	

Real Estate Records	Where to Find It
Cemetery deed	
Deeds	
Easements	
Home improvement records	
Leases	

Real Estate Records	Where to Find It
Mortgages	
Reverse mortgage	
Tax records	
Timeshare agreements	
Other	
Other	
Other	

Other Asset and Debt Records	Where to Find It
Business records	
Computers	
Copyright documentation	
Credit card contracts	
Jewelry inventory/appraisals	
Loans and notes	
Patents and trademarks documentation	
Personal property inventory	
Rare books	
Vehicle titles	
Warranties	

End of Life Planning	Where to Find It
Body donation papers	
Celebration of life prearrangements	
Cemetery deed	
Cremation prearrangement agreement	
Ethical will	
Funeral prearrangement agreement	
Health care directives	
Legacy information	
Letters of instruction	
Letters to be sent on death	
List of people to contact upon death	
Living will	
Mausoleum deed	
Obituary	
Organ donor card	
Pet continuing care	
Trust	
Will	
Other	
Other	
Other	

Personal History: Other Highlights

CHAPTER 2
MY FAMILY HISTORY

Information about your family history is precious—and easily lost. With each passing generation, it becomes harder to track down when a distant relative settled in this country or where a favorite grandparent is buried. In this chapter, you can do a little digging to learn about your family while building a richer legacy for the next generation.

This chapter gives you a place to record as much of your family history as you can gather, person by person. Take a first pass, filling in what you know. Make gathering the rest of the answers an enjoyable fact-finding adventure.

My To-Do Checklist

Done	Need to Do	
❑	❑	Take advantage of family gatherings and one-on-one exchanges to compile your family history
❑	❑	Conduct other research to fill in the blanks
❑	❑	Be sensitive about collecting your family medical history
❑	❑	Complete the checklists for Chapter 2

✔ Take advantage of family gatherings and one-on-one exchanges to compile your family history

To learn about your family, talk to relatives at events. Telephone, drop a note to, e-mail, or visit your grandparents, parents, aunts, uncles, siblings, and children to gradually complete your family's history. Even if you're not close, reach out. As a bonus, you may even rekindle family ties.

Checklists are provided for multiple relatives, but you can modify the lists to suit your needs. (The digital checklists, downloadable at **ambar.org/AARPforms**, are easy to modify.) For example, you might want to add sections for stepparents, multiple cousins, and great-aunts and -uncles; delete the section on siblings if you're an only child; or add the term "significant other" or "life partner."

Use the space for notes as you wish. You might tell stories about a relative's immigration to this country, career highlights, or meals you've shared. While you are searching out information about your relatives, this is a good time to note when and where they were born and, if they've passed on, when and how they died.

✔ Conduct additional research to fill in the blanks

You may be able to find some missing details on birth and death certificates, census records, and obituaries. Online genealogical sites can also be helpful resources to track down missing information about your ancestors. You have space to write personal notes about your relatives. Use the space as you wish. For example, you can give a brief history, explain a relative's beliefs or accomplishments, or share personal reminiscences. Here is a place to pass on those special moments you shared with a grandparent or the funny story about your brother when you were kids.

✔ Be sensitive about gathering your family medical history

The Family Medical History checklist provides a place to note the illnesses and conditions your relatives have. It's a simple check-off list, with places to fill in details.

Some family members, understandably, may be unwilling to share medical information. Find a private place to talk. Explain why you want to know about their health and how it will help you and others in your family. Tell them that the Family Medical History checklist could prove valuable in the diagnosis, early treatment, and, in some cases, prevention of certain hereditary medical conditions. You and your family can use this information to identify illnesses or medical conditions that run in your family.

By noticing health patterns among relatives, healthcare professionals can determine whether you, other family members, or future generations may be at an increased risk of developing a particular condition. A family medical history can identify people with a higher-than-usual chance of having common disorders, such as heart disease, high blood pressure, stroke, certain cancers, and diabetes. It also can provide information about the risk of rarer conditions caused by mutations in a single gene, such as cystic fibrosis and sickle cell disease. Knowing your family medical history allows you to take steps to reduce your risk. You may want more frequent screening (such as mammography or colonoscopy) starting at an earlier age, or you may schedule regular checkups or testing for a medical condition that runs in your family. That said, you will need to respect the privacy of anyone who is not comfortable revealing this information.

FAMILY HISTORY ACTION CHECKLISTS

In the other chapters, the checklists are in alphabetical order, but in this chapter they're listed by family members in order of how they might inherit if you do not have a will. (This is called intestate succession, which you'll learn more about in Chapter 8.)

The checklists in Chapter 2 are set out in the following order:

- *Children and Grandchildren*
- *Parents*
- *Siblings*
- *Grandparents*
- *Aunts, Uncles, and Cousins*
- *Family Medical History*
- *Family History: Other Highlights*

You can download these checklists in Word or fillable PDF format at **ambar.org/AARPforms**.

Children and Grandchildren

Name at present: ______________________________

Name at birth (if different): ______________________________

Phone: ______________ E-mail: ______________________________

Address: ______________________________

Favorite memories:

____

____

____

____

____

____

Place of birth: ______________________________
City *County* *State* *Country*

Place of burial: ______________________________

Cause of death: ______________________________

Marital status:

- ❑ Never married
- ❑ Currently married
- ❑ Married ______ times

	Name of Spouse	Date of Marriage	Date of Divorce	Date of Death
# 1				
# 2				

Number of children: ______________

	Name of Child	Date of Birth	Date of Death
# 1			
# 2			
# 3			
# 4			

****

Name at present: ______________________________

Name at birth (if different): ______________________________

Phone: ______________ E-mail: ______________

Address: ______________________________

Favorite memories:

____

____

____

____

____

____

Place of birth: ______________________________
City *County* *State* *Country*

Place of burial: ______________________________

Cause of death: ______________________________

Marital status:

- ❑ Never married
- ❑ Currently married
- ❑ Married ______ times

	Name of Spouse	Date of Marriage	Date of Divorce	Date of Death
# 1				
# 2				

Number of children: ________________

	Name of Child	Date of Birth	Date of Death
# 1			
# 2			
# 3			
# 4			

****

Name at present: ____

Name at birth (if different): ____________________________________

Phone: ______________________ E-mail: ________________________

Address: ____

Favorite memories:

____

____

____

____

____

____

Place of birth: ____
City *County* *State* *Country*

Place of burial: ____

Cause of death: ____

Marital status:

❑ Never married

❑ Currently married

❑ Married ______ times

	Name of Spouse	Date of Marriage	Date of Divorce	Date of Death
# 1				
# 2				

Number of children: _______________

	Name of Child	Date of Birth	Date of Death
# 1			
# 2			
# 3			
# 4			

****

Name at present: ____

Name at birth (if different): __________________________________

Phone: ____________________ E-mail: _________________________

Address: ____

Favorite memories:

____

____

____

____

____

____

Place of birth: ____

City *County* *State* *Country*

Place of burial: ____

Cause of death: ____

Marital status:

- ❑ Never married
- ❑ Currently married
- ❑ Married ______ times

	Name of Spouse	Date of Marriage	Date of Divorce	Date of Death
# 1				
# 2				

Number of children: _______________

	Name of Child	Date of Birth	Date of Death
# 1			
# 2			
# 3			
# 4			

Parents

Name: ______________________________

Phone: ________________ E-mail: ________________

Address: ______________________________

Date of birth: ____________ Place of birth: ________________

Date of death: ____________ Cause of death: ________________

Favorite memories:

____

____

____

____

____

____

____

____

____

____

____

____

____

____

____

Name: ______________________________

Phone: ______________ E-mail: ______________

Address: ______________________________

Date of birth: ______________ Place of birth: ______________

Date of death: ______________ Cause of death: ______________

Favorite memories:

____

____

____

____

____

____

____

____

____

____

____

____

____

____

____

Siblings

Name at present: ______________________________

Name at birth (if different): ______________________________

Phone: ____________________ E-mail: ______________________________

Address: ______________________________

Favorite memories:

____

____

____

____

Date of birth: ______________________________

Place of birth: ______________________________
City *County* *State* *Country*

Date of death: ________________ Cause of death: ______________________________

Place of burial: ______________________________

Marital status:

- ❑ Never married
- ❑ Currently married
- ❑ Married ______ times

	Name of Spouse	Date of Marriage	Date of Divorce	Date of Death
# 1				
# 2				

Number of children: _______________

	Name of Child	Date of Birth	Date of Death
# 1			
# 2			
# 3			
# 4			

****

Name at present: ____

Name at birth (if different): ____________________________________

Phone: ____________________ E-mail: ______________________________

Address: ____

Favorite memories:

____

____

____

____

Date of birth: ____

Place of birth: ____

City *County* *State* *Country*

Date of death: ________________ Cause of death: ______________________

Place of burial: ____

Marital status:

- ❑ Never married
- ❑ Currently married
- ❑ Married ______ times

	Name of Spouse	Date of Marriage	Date of Divorce	Date of Death
# 1				
# 2				

Number of children: ________________

	Name of Child	Date of Birth	Date of Death
# 1			
# 2			
# 3			
# 4			

****

Name at present: ____

Name at birth (if different): ____________________________________

Phone: ____________________ E-mail: _________________________________

Address: ____

Favorite memories:

____

____

____

____

Date of birth: ____

Place of birth: ____
City *County* *State* *Country*

Date of death: ______________ Cause of death: ______________________

Place of burial: ____

Marital status:

- ❑ Never married
- ❑ Currently married
- ❑ Married ______ times

	Name of Spouse	Date of Marriage	Date of Divorce	Date of Death
# 1				
# 2				

Number of children: ______________

	Name of Child	Date of Birth	Date of Death
# 1			
# 2			
# 3			
# 4			

****

Name at present: ____

Name at birth (if different): ________________________________

Phone: ____________________ E-mail: ______________________________

Address: ____

Favorite memories:

____

____

____

____

Date of birth: ____

Place of birth: ____
City *County* *State* *Country*

Date of death: ________________ Cause of death: ______________________

Place of burial: ____

Marital status:

- ❑ Never married
- ❑ Currently married
- ❑ Married ______ times

	Name of Spouse	Date of Marriage	Date of Divorce	Date of Death
# 1				
# 2				

Number of children: _______________

	Name of Child	Date of Birth	Date of Death
# 1			
# 2			
# 3			
# 4			

Grandparents

Name: ______________________________

- ❑ Paternal grandfather ❑ Paternal grandmother
- ❑ Maternal grandfather ❑ Maternal grandmother

Phone: ______________ E-mail: ______________

Address: ______________________________

Date of birth: ______________ Place of birth: ______________

Date of death: ______________ Cause of death: ______________

Favorite memories:

____

____

____

____

Name: ______________________________

- ❑ Paternal grandfather ❑ Paternal grandmother
- ❑ Maternal grandfather ❑ Maternal grandmother

Phone: ______________ E-mail: ______________

Address: ______________________________

Date of birth: ______________ Place of birth: ______________

Date of death: ______________ Cause of death: ______________

Favorite memories:

____

____

____

____

Name: __________________________________

❑ Paternal grandfather ❑ Paternal grandmother

❑ Maternal grandfather ❑ Maternal grandmother

Phone: ________________ E-mail: ____________________

Address: __________________________________

Date of birth: ____________ Place of birth: ________________

Date of death: ____________ Cause of death: ________________

Favorite memories:

____

____

____

____

Name: ______________________________

- ❑ Paternal grandfather
- ❑ Paternal grandmother
- ❑ Maternal grandfather
- ❑ Maternal grandmother

Phone: ____________________ E-mail: ____________________

Address: ______________________________

Date of birth: ________________ Place of birth: ____________________

Date of death: ________________ Cause of death: ____________________

Favorite memories:

____

____

____

____

Aunts, Uncles, and Cousins

Name: ____

How this person is related to me: ______________________________

Phone: ____________________ E-mail: __________________________

Address: ____

Date of birth: ______________ Place of birth: ____________________

Date of death: ______________ Cause of death: ___________________

Favorite memories:

____

____

____

____

Name: ____

How this person is related to me: ______________________________

Phone: ____________________ E-mail: __________________________

Address: ____

Date of birth: ______________ Place of birth: ____________________

Date of death: ______________ Cause of death: ___________________

Favorite memories:

____

____

____

____

Name: ______________________________

How this person is related to me: ______________________________

Phone: ______________ E-mail: ______________

Address: ______________________________

Date of birth: ______________ Place of birth: ______________

Date of death: ______________ Cause of death: ______________

Favorite memories:

____

____

____

____

Name: ______________________________

How this person is related to me: ______________________________

Phone: ______________ E-mail: ______________

Address: ______________________________

Date of birth: ______________ Place of birth: ______________

Date of death: ______________ Cause of death: ______________

Favorite memories:

____

____

____

____

Name: ______________________________

How this person is related to me: ______________________________

Phone: ______________ E-mail: ______________

Address: ______________________________

Date of birth: ______________ Place of birth: ______________

Date of death: ______________ Cause of death: ______________

Favorite memories:

____

____

____

____

Name: ______________________________

How this person is related to me: ______________________________

Phone: ______________ E-mail: ______________________________

Address: ______________________________

Date of birth: ______________ Place of birth: ______________________________

Date of death: ______________ Cause of death: ______________________________

Favorite memories:

____

____

____

____

Name: ______________________________

How this person is related to me: ______________________________

Phone: ______________ E-mail: ______________________________

Address: ______________________________

Date of birth: ______________ Place of birth: ______________________________

Date of death: ______________ Cause of death: ______________________________

Favorite memories:

____

____

____

____

Name: ____

How this person is related to me: ______________________________

Phone: ____________________ E-mail: ____________________________

Address: ____

Date of birth: ______________ Place of birth: __________________

Date of death: ______________ Cause of death: _________________

Favorite memories:

____

____

____

____

Family Medical History

Medical conditions in my family (including parents, grandparents, siblings, uncles, aunts, and children):

Condition	Who	Details
❑ Alcoholism		
❑ Allergies		
❑ Alzheimer's disease		
❑ Arthritis		
❑ Asthma		
❑ Birth defects		
❑ Blood disorder		
❑ Cancer		
❑ Chromosomal disorder		
❑ Cystic fibrosis		
❑ Dementia		
❑ Depression		
❑ Diabetes Type 1		
❑ Diabetes Type 2		
❑ Drug addiction		
❑ Eczema		
❑ Endometriosis		
❑ Epilepsy		

Condition	Who	Details
❑ Gallbladder problems		
❑ Gastrointestinal disorders		
❑ Glaucoma		
❑ Gout		
❑ Hay fever		
❑ Hearing loss		
❑ Heart disease		
❑ High blood pressure		
❑ High cholesterol		
❑ Infertility		
❑ Inflammatory bowel disease		
❑ Intellectual disabilities		
❑ Kidney disease		
❑ Learning disabilities		
❑ Lung disease		
❑ Lymphoma		
❑ Mental disorder		
❑ Miscarriage or stillbirth		
❑ Muscular dystrophy		
❑ Neurological disorders		

Condition	Who	Details
❑ Obesity		
❑ Osteoporosis		
❑ Post-Traumatic Stress Disorder		
❑ Psoriasis		
❑ Sickle cell disease		
❑ Skin cancer: basal cell		
❑ Skin cancer: melanoma		
❑ Skin cancer: squamous cell		
❑ Stomach disorders		
❑ Stroke		
❑ Thyroid disorder		
❑ Ulcers		
❑ Vision impairment		
❑ Other		
❑ Other		

Notes about my family's medical history:

____

____

____

____

Family History: Other Highlights

CHAPTER 3
MY INSURANCE

This chapter moves beyond collecting personal and family information to reviewing and gathering your insurance information. It's helpful to have your insurance details and documents organized in one place so you can keep track of your coverage and payments. And, if something happens to you—death, an accident, a stroke, or other event that prevents you from continuing to conduct your own financial affairs—your loved ones will need that information to file insurance claims, pay premiums, cancel certain policies, or obtain new ones to protect you, your family, and your property. To take advantage of any insurance that you have obtained, your family needs to know about all your different kinds of insurance policies. Millions of dollars of life insurance proceeds go unclaimed because the policyholder's family was never told about them.

Some people find it irritating to see all those insurance costs in one place. Indeed, I often hear people complain about the high price of insurance. On the other hand, I've heard stories of how insurance provided life-saving cancer treatments for children or rebuilt a home destroyed by a fire. Personally, I was glad I had insurance when the heirloom necklace I wore at my wedding was later stolen and when my car suddenly caught on fire while driving the interstate. The payment of premiums protects us (to the limits of the policy) against financial losses caused by illness, accidents, fire, and theft, depending on the type of insurance purchased. Any loss is shared by all of those insured, saving the individual from financial ruin.

Health insurance, for instance, can save us paying the high cost of medical care. Homeowners insurance can save us tens of thousands of dollars in case of fire and other disasters as well as theft. In this chapter, you'll pull together all your policies—for example, health care coverage, with perhaps separate policies for prescription drugs, vision, and dental, maybe through your employer or through Medicare, Medicare Part D prescription drug coverage, and a Medicare Advantage plan. However you mix and match your medical coverage, the checklists in this chapter will help you track what premiums are due when, how you pay those premiums, what is covered, contact information for the agent or company, and when and how you can make any changes to your policy as your circumstances and the insurance coverage change.

This chapter also gives you an opportunity to make sure you have the insurance coverage you need. To that end, I offer brief overviews of the types of insurance available. Skip over whatever isn't applicable. While I don't provide comprehensive details of the many types of insurance options available, the summaries should give you enough to consider what you need—and don't need. Always check with a professional about your needs for your situation.

My To-Do Checklist

Done	Need to Do	
❑	❑	Understand and annually review your health insurance, including Medicare
❑	❑	Be alert to Medicaid eligibility requirements
❑	❑	Keep your vehicle insurance current
❑	❑	Review your homeowners or renters insurance coverage
❑	❑	Review the terms of your life insurance and annuity policies
❑	❑	Understand long-term care insurance and review your policy
❑	❑	Update the beneficiaries you have listed on all your policies
❑	❑	Complete the checklists for Chapter 3

✔ Understand and annually review your health insurance, including Medicare

Considering the high cost of health care, you'll want to keep close track of your health insurance, whether through your employer or other group coverage, a private company, or government programs like Medicare and Marketplace Plans. Your plan's coverage and prices likely change every year.

You need to know whether you have the right coverage at a price you can afford, what your options are if you want to make a change in coverage, and when the window of opportunity is open to make any changes. Adding to the complexity of navigating the health insurance maze are all the possible types of coverage: hospitalization, medical and mental health services, drugs, vision, and dental.

More than half the people in the United States people get health insurance as an employee benefit where they work. The employer pays part of the premiums and deducts the workers' share of the premium from their paycheck. Upon retirement, some people can continue to get health coverage through their former employer's health plan. Employers aren't required to provide retiree health insurance and can cut or eliminate those benefits at any time. Check with your employer's benefits coordinator about the health insurance benefits available to you.

Typically, with group health insurance you have an opportunity each year to modify your coverage. You should watch for any "open season" announcements as plan options and coverage frequently change.

Less than 10 percent of Americans don't have health insurance. If you fall in that category, you can obtain coverage through the Health Insurance Marketplace in your state. The Marketplace at healthcare.gov is a way to shop and sign up for health insurance that allows side-by-side comparison of the benefits and costs of health plans available from approved private health insurance companies. All health plans sold in the Marketplace must cover basic health benefits, including doctor visits, hospitalization, mental health services, and prescription drugs. You can pick among several levels of coverage at different prices. Financial assistance to pay the premiums may be available, depending on your income. You pay your premium directly to the insurance company, not the government.

Medicare is a government health insurance program for those who are age 65 and older, younger people with a qualifying disability, and people with end-stage kidney disease. There are whole books on this topic (including AARP's *Medicare for Dummies*), but this chapter offers you a brief overview. You'll want to enroll for Medicare on time or you'll pay penalties. (The exception is people already receiving Social Security or Railroad Retirement benefits; they are automatically enrolled.) Penalties are steep: 10 percent more in premiums for each 12-month period that you could have had Medicare but didn't sign up for it, and those premium hikes stay in effect.

So as you approach your 65th birthday—even if you are still working or receiving health insurance from a former employer—do your research on when to enroll, how your current coverage and Medicare work together, and all your options. And like other health insurance, you'll need to review your Medicare plans each year and, if you choose to, change plans during the limited open season.

Medicare has several parts that provide different benefits. Premiums and income limits are as of 2022.

Part A helps pay for inpatient hospital care, preventive screenings, hospice care, some home health care, and a limited amount of skilled nursing care. Most people don't pay premiums for Part A coverage because they have already been paid for through payroll taxes. For those who need to purchase Part A, the monthly premium is $274 or $499 (as of 2022), depending on how long you or your spouse worked and paid Medicare taxes.

Part B helps pay for part of the costs for doctor visits, some home health care, medical equipment, preventive services, outpatient hospital care, rehabilitative therapy, laboratory tests, X-rays, mental health services, ambulance services, and blood transfusions.

Medicare beneficiaries pay a premium for Part B. In 2022, the premium is $170.10 each month for people with income under $91,000 for an individual or $182,000 for a married couple filing jointly. People who earn more pay premiums up to $578.30 (as of 2022). This additional premium, called the income-related monthly adjustment amount or IRMAA, is based on the modified adjusted gross income reported on the income tax return filed the previous year. For example, the 2022 premium would be based on the income tax return filed in 2021 for 2020 income. The premium can be adjusted if your income has significantly decreased due to a life-changing event such as death of a spouse, marriage, divorce, or work stoppage. If you think you should not be paying an increased premium, make an appointment to speak with a claims representative at your local Social Security office or file form SSA-44, available at www.ssa.gov/forms/ssa-44-ext.pdf.

As noted, if you don't sign up in the allotted window, you'll pay a penalty. There is an exception if you are covered by another policy, such as your employer's or former employer's plan, although your retiree health plan may require that you enroll in Parts A and B.

If you have retiree benefits plus Medicare, you need to know how the two work together. If you're under 65 when you retire, your retiree health plan will be your primary coverage. Check with your human relations department for the details about spouse and family coverage, premium amounts, and health services that are offered, including dental and vision. For those of you 65 and older and eligible for Medicare along with a retiree plan, you may have additional questions. I know I sure did, but I got them answered and now have it figured out.

I have retiree benefits from my last employer as well as Medicare. For me, Medicare is primary; my retiree coverage is secondary. This means that the doctor or pharmacy first bills Medicare and then my retiree health plan. Generally, my retiree health plan pays some or most of what Medicare didn't cover. Each time I go to the doctor or pharmacy, I make sure it has all my plan information and numbers.

If your employer or retiree coverage ends, you have eight months to sign up for Part B. After that eight-month deadline, you'll pay a penalty of increased premiums for the rest of your life.

How to pay your Medicare Part A and Part B premiums? If you receive Social Security, your premiums are automatically deducted from your monthly Social Security benefit. Otherwise, you can pay online through your Medicare account, use your bank's direct bill pay services, mail a check, or sign up for Medicare Easy Pay at cms.gov/medicare/cms-forms/cms-forms/downloads/sf5510english.pdf to have your premiums automatically deducted from a bank account. When I enrolled in Medicare, I signed up for Medicare Easy Pay, but it took several months to get the automatic payments started. I continued to mail a check each month until I got the notice that my premium was being deducted.

If you need help paying the Part A deductible, coinsurance, and copayments and Part B premiums and deductibles, check out the ***Medicare Savings Programs***. Depending on your income, you may qualify for state programs that pay some of the premium or deductibles. A good place to get personal help understanding Medicare and Medicare Savings Programs is your local State Health Insurance Assistance Program (SHIP). To find the SHIP in your state, go to https://acl.gov/programs/connecting-people-services/state-health-insurance-assistance-program-ship ("State Health Insurance Assistance Program (SHIP) | ACL Administration for Community Living").

Part C is now known as ***Medicare Advantage***. You have the option to purchase a Medicare Advantage plan, which is offered by private insurance companies. These policies pay for the same services as Parts A and B and may offer additional benefits such as drug, dental, or vision coverage. In most Medicare Advantage plans, participants can go only to doctors, specialists, and hospitals that are on the plan's list of providers. If you want to change to a different Medicare Advantage plan or select original Medicare (that is, Part A and Part B), you can do so during the annual Medicare open enrollment periods between October 15 and December 7. You can also change from one Medicare Advantage Plan to another between January 1 and March 31.

Moving is one of the key reasons to consider a change, and there is a Special Enrollment Period for that purpose—from one month before to two months after you move. You'll need to check if your Advantage plan is available in the new service area; some plans don't have provider networks in every state.

Compare Medicare Advantage plans at www.medicare.gov/plan-compare ("Find a Medicare Plan"). You pay your premiums directly to the Advantage plan insurer.

Part D helps pay for prescription drugs. Like Medicare Advantage plans, Part D drug coverage is optional and offered through private insurance companies approved by Medicare. Some Advantage plans include prescription drug coverage. If so, you don't need a separate Part D plan.

People already on Medicare Parts A and B can choose from many Part D drug plans offered by many companies. The benefits and costs vary among insurance companies and each company's several plans. Your first opportunity to elect to purchase Part D drug coverage is when you become newly eligible for Medicare; wait too long, and again, you'll pay a late enrollment penalty. You can switch Part D plans or sign up for a Part D plan during the annual Medicare open enrollment period (October 15 through December 5). If you have income over $88,000 for an individual, $176,000 for a couple filing a joint return, you have to pay an additional $12.30 to $77.10 (as of 2021) to Medicare on top of the regular Part D premium you pay to the plan.

As with most other insurance plans, in addition to premiums, Medicare has an annual deductible, coinsurance, and copayments. Supplemental insurance called ***Medigap*** is designed to cover some of the costs that aren't paid by Medicare. (But note that Medigap doesn't work with Medicare Advantage Plans and, in fact, it's illegal for someone to try to sell you a Medigap policy if you are on an Advantage Plan.) Medigap is private health insurance offered by Medicare-approved insurance companies that can offer up to ten standardized plans. Each standard plan offers a different set of benefits, fills different gaps in Medicare coverage, and varies in price. The standardization of plans makes it easier to compare policies among companies. Use the tool at www.medicare.gov/medigap-supplemental-insurance-plans to compare Medigap policies. Keep in mind that they never cover vision, dental, hearing aids, eyeglasses, private-duty nursing, or long-term care.

Compare the various Medicare plans, including prescription drug, Medicare Advantage, and Medigap at medicare.gov/find-a-plan. To sign up for Medicare, go to ssa.gov/medicare/apply.html. To readily track Medicare claims and payments, sign up for a personal account at MyMedicare.gov.

Once you are on Medicare, pay close attention to the ***Medicare Summary Notices*** (MSN), which explain Medicare's action on claims that health care providers have filed to your account. MSNs come by mail, or you can set up an account at MyMedicare.gov, where claims are posted within about a day of being processed. The MSN, which prominently says "This is not a bill," contains important information about the provider that filed a claim; the service provided; the amount Medicare paid; and the amount, if any, the provider can bill the patient.

To make sure your bills are processed accurately, compare the information on the MSN with the provider's statement and the insurance company's claim form for each visit (which all come at different times) to make sure the information matches. If you see anything that doesn't look right, like you paid a doctor a higher copayment than Medicare calculated, first contact the provider. It could be a simple mistake that the provider can correct. For bigger problems or suspected fraud, contact Medicare at 800-663-4227. The Medical Claims Tracker checklist in this chapter is a handy tool to organize your claims information.

✔ Be alert to Medicaid eligibility requirements

Medicaid is a federal benefit program managed by the states that provides health care coverage based on financial need. Some 75 million people received Medicaid in 2019, according to the Centers for Medicare and Medicaid Services. Unlike Medicare, which pays for a very limited amount of long-term care, Medicaid will pay almost all the cost of nursing home care. More than 60 percent of nursing home residents were supported primarily by Medicaid in 2019, according to the Centers for Disease Control and Prevention.

Medicaid rules are rather complicated and can vary in detail from state to state. In a nutshell, to qualify for Medicaid (as of 2021), individuals have to have very low income and less than $2,000 (in most states) in assets. Your car, personal possessions, up to $500,000 of the value of your home, and money to pay for your funeral don't count in determining your assets. Married couples have different rules that vary from state to state. If you need to go into a nursing home, you must spend your money (income and assets) until you get down to the asset limit before you can apply for Medicaid. When you apply, Medicaid looks back at how you've spent your money the last five years. The "look back period" is meant to prevent Medicaid applicants from giving away assets or selling them for less than market value in an attempt to meet Medicaid's asset limit. Making a significant gift to someone other than your spouse within five years of your application is considered "a transfer for less than fair market value" and may delay your eligibility. This eligibility penalty is calculated by dividing the value of the transfer by the state's average nursing facility private pay rate to determine how many months you have to wait before you are eligible for Medicaid. Say you've given your child $24,000 in the past five years, and the average nursing home rate is $6,000 a month. You'd divide $24,000 by $6000, resulting in a four-month delay in eligibility. Every state has different rate. You can find your state's rate at the American Council on Aging's "State Specific Medicaid Eligibility Requirements," www.medicaid planningassistance.org/state-specific-medicaid-eligibility.

Because Medicaid rules are so complicated and vary from state to state, consult with a lawyer who is well versed on Medicaid in your state before making any significant gifts.

✔ Keep your vehicle insurance current

If you own a motor vehicle—car, truck, motorcycle, motorboat, snowmobile, RV, or other vehicle—you probably have vehicle insurance. In fact, many states require all drivers to be insured for liability to other people for damages resulting from an accident. Regardless of the law in your particular state, it makes good sense to insure yourself against the claims by others and against any expenses that you might have if you have a collision or your vehicle is stolen.

Review your policies to make sure the coverage is accurate. When I retired and stopped commuting to my office every day, I started driving many fewer miles. (Hooray, one of the many perks of retirement!) I explained the change in my driving routine to my insurance agent and got a discount by switching from commuter use to personal use. You should also check to see if your policy includes coverage for any person, family member or not, who is driving your car with your permission. If other people are going to use the car routinely, such as a housekeeper or home health aide, it's good to add their names to the policy.

✔ Review your homeowners or renters insurance coverage

Originally, fire insurance was about the only type of insurance that homeowners could obtain on their residence. Now you can get insurance to protect against windstorm, hail, flood, explosion, smoke damage, and more. Insurance might cover not only the building but also the repair or replacement of the contents in your home, as well as your garage or any outbuildings.

Today, most homeowners purchase a homeowners policy that combines fire and extended insurance coverage that also includes protection for your personal property, additional living expenses if you can't live in your home because of damage, and comprehensive personal liability that would cover medical payments to guests who get injured in your home and damage to other's property. Similar types of policies are available to condominium owners. Renters can purchase insurance policies that cover personal property due to damage to the unit. You can also add ***riders*** or ***endorsements*** to your policy to fit specific needs or to insure special items such as antiques or jewelry. I collect vintage pottery, for instance, and have a rider for that. As soon as I acquire a new piece, I send a brief description and photo to my insurance agent and ask that it be added to my list of covered property.

Now is a good time to check the declarations on your homeowners policy to verify that you have the right coverage. Look to see if you have actual cash value coverage or replacement cost coverage. It can make a big difference in how much you will receive if you need to make a claim. An actual cash value policy will pay you what the insurance company determines is the depreciated value to repair or replace the item. Replacement cost coverage pays you what it would cost today to get a similar item. So, for example, if you make a claim on a cash value policy for a fire-damaged kitchen with fifteen-year-old appliances, you'll get much less than what it costs to buy new appliances of similar quality. For both, you'll also have to account for deductibles—the amount you pay before you get any coverage—and limits—the maximum amount the company will pay in total. If it has been a while since you purchased your homeowners policy and you have made significant upgrades to your property, you may want to up your coverage. As I explain in Chapter 9, it's a good idea to have a photo or video inventory of your personal possessions to prove what you own in case you need to make an insurance claim.

Many insurance companies offer additional insurance liability protection through an ***umbrella policy***, which provides insurance coverage over and above your regular automobile, personal liability, and other liability coverage. It is usually sold in multiples of $1 million and can be a low-cost method of buying substantial protection.

✔ Review the terms of your life insurance and annuity policies

Life insurance is primarily intended to ease the financial loss to a beneficiary that results from the policyholder's death, providing financial support to your spouse or dependent children after your die. Life insurance is also a way to help your family pay for your final expenses, such as those incurred during any final illness, a funeral, estate taxes, or unpaid debts.

Today's life insurance market has multiple options for you to choose from, including how much coverage you purchase (that is, how much your beneficiaries will receive), the cost of the premiums, how your payments are invested, any guarantees on returns, and how and when the policy proceeds are paid out to your beneficiaries. You can choose how the proceeds are paid (in a lump sum, a monthly sum for the life of another individual, or monthly sums over a certain length of time). The amount your beneficiary will receive may even pay double if your death is caused by accident—a so-called ***double indemnity*** policy. Because there are so many options when obtaining life insurance, be certain you understand all the benefits and risks involved. If you don't understand the coverage you currently have or are considering, ask questions until you do. Compare your choices with multiple insurance companies to make sure you have the coverage you want and need.

These are the primary forms of life insurance:

- ***Whole life insurance*** is a widely purchased type of insurance that pays a sum of money (the "face value") to your beneficiary at the time of your death. You pay a premium each year to keep the insurance in force. The amount of the premium is determined by your age at the time you purchase the policy. The younger you are, the less expensive the premium. Some employers and organizations offer group coverage, which may lower the premiums and avoid the need to pass a qualifying physical examination, called proof of insurability. Variations in the method of payment for whole life insurance are available. For example, you might obtain a policy that requires annual premiums for 20 years; at the expiration of the 20-year period, you stop paying premiums, but your policy remains in effect for the balance of your life. Or you can purchase a policy by making one large initial premium payment. Regardless of how you pay for the policy, whole life insurance provides coverage for life (thus the name "whole life"), provided you've paid all the required premiums on time.

- ***Universal life, variable whole life, and variable universal life*** are terms used to describe other types of whole life insurance policies in which you have the option to vary (within the terms of the contract) the amount you pay in premiums from year to year and the way your policy's cash reserves grow. Typically, the cash value reserves held by the insurance company are invested in stocks, bonds, or mutual funds. You, as the policyholder, select the investments from a menu offered by the insurance company. Some policies have guaranteed minimum returns on the investment; others allow you to borrow against the cash value during your life. The amount your beneficiary would receive at your death varies based on many factors, including the terms of the policy, the amounts paid in premiums, and the investment success of the insurance company.
- ***Term insurance***, as opposed to whole life insurance, provides coverage for only a specified length of time. You might purchase a policy that provides coverage for five years, ten years, or twenty years. The annual premium is substantially less than the annual premium for whole life insurance. The cost of purchasing the same amount of coverage gradually increases with your age. Many term life insurance contracts provide that the policy may be renewed at the end of the term without proof that your health has not changed, although your premium will likely be higher than for the original term because you would be older. Other term policies provide that they may be converted, within a certain period, into whole life insurance without proof of insurability. Once again, the premium would be adjusted.

Annuities are a type of insurance coverage typically designed to provide a stream of income. There are many types of annuities: fixed, variable, or indexed, with immediate or deferred payments. Typically, money invested in the annuity grows tax-deferred, meaning you aren't taxed on any interest earned until you receive a payment, presumably when your tax rate is lower in retirement.

When choosing an annuity, you'll likely have many options, including how your money is invested within the annuity, at what point your annuity begins to make payments, and to whom payments will be made. You'll also choose whether payouts will be made for a fixed number of years, or during your lifetime, or for the lifetime of a spouse or other beneficiary. You can also obtain, at additional cost, specific benefits, such as a guaranteed minimum death benefit (GMDB) or a guaranteed minimum withdrawal benefit (GMWB). With a guaranteed minimum death benefit, your beneficiaries or your estate will receive a set amount as defined in the contract if you die before the annuity begins paying benefits. A guaranteed minimum withdrawal benefit means that while you are alive, you will receive a fixed percentage of your investment each year. Be certain you understand the terms of any annuity you have and periodically review your annuity contract to confirm that it continues to fit your needs. While you are reviewing your annuity, make sure that the beneficiary information is up to date.

✔ Locate your life insurance policies

Regardless of the type of life insurance you hold, keep your life insurance policies in a safe place and be sure your family knows where they are located, should something happen to you. Some companies may require that your family hand over the original life insurance policy before they pay any proceeds. You may want to have two copies of each policy: the original in your safe deposit box and a copy at home with other important legal documents.

Be sure to note on the Where to Find It checklist where you are safekeeping any life insurance policies. Because missing a premium payment can cause the cancellation of the policy and the loss of all the premiums that you have previously invested, record on the Life Insurance checklist when premiums are due and the amount of the premium, or whether the policy is paid in full.

✔ Understand long-term care insurance and review your policy

If you have a long-term care insurance policy, now might be a good time to review your coverage to help cover potential long-term care expenses. If you don't have a policy, a financial adviser or a lawyer who specializes in elder law or estate planning can advise you about ways to save for future long-term care expenses and the pros and cons of purchasing long-term care insurance. In this section, I'll give you a general overview.

Depending on the policy options you select, long-term care insurance can help you pay for the care you need, whether you are living in your own home or in an assisted living or skilled nursing community. The insurance might also pay expenses for care coordination and other services. Some policies will even help pay costs associated with modifying your home so you can keep living in it safely.

Here are some factors to consider when reviewing your existing policy or purchasing a new one.

Your age and health. Policies cost less if purchased when you're younger and in good health. If you're older or have a serious health condition, you may not be able to get coverage—and if you do, your costs may be considerably higher. Insurers often turn down applicants due to preexisting conditions. If a company does sell a policy to someone with preexisting conditions, it often withholds payment for care related to those conditions for a specified time after the policy is purchased. Make sure this period of withheld payments is reasonable for you. If you fail to notify a company of a preexisting condition, the company may not pay for care related to that condition.

The premiums. Premiums often increase over time, and your income may go down. If you find yourself unable to afford the premiums, you could lose all the money you've invested in a policy. Contact the company to find out if you can change or reduce coverage that will lower the premiums and save your investment in the policy. If you need to stop paying your premium or drop your benefit, check to see if your policy has a "nonforfeiture option." This option allows you to receive a reduced amount of coverage based on the amount of money you've already paid. Some states require policies to offer nonforfeiture benefits, including benefit options with different premiums. Since nonforfeiture provisions vary by location, check with your state's insurance department or your state's listing at your SHIP before dropping your policy. If your policy doesn't have a nonforfeiture option and you stop paying the premiums, you'll lose all the benefits for which you have paid. Be sure to note on the checklist in this chapter how much you pay in premiums, when they are due, and how you pay them. You don't want to have your policy lapse through an overlooked payment.

Being able to continue to afford the premiums after retirement is a barrier for many people thinking about getting long-term care policies. Companies can't single you out for a rate increase, but they can increase rates on all similar policies sold in your state.

Your income. If you have difficulty paying your bills now or are concerned about paying them in the years ahead when you may have less income and fewer assets, spending thousands of dollars a year for a long-term care policy might not make sense. If your income is low and you have few assets when you need care, you might qualify for Medicaid. Medicaid pays for nursing facility care; in most states it will also cover a limited amount of at-home care. Unfortunately, to be eligible for Medicaid benefits you must first exhaust almost all your resources and meet Medicaid's other strict eligibility requirements. I explain these Medicaid eligibility requirements beginning on page 78.

Regarding Medicaid, if you purchase a long-term care insurance policy that qualifies for the State Partnership Program, you can keep a specified amount of resources over the resource limit and still qualify for Medicaid. Most states have a State Partnership Program. Be sure to ask your insurance agent whether the policy you're considering qualifies under the State Partnership Program and how it works with Medicaid. You can find out more about this program from the Administration for Community Living at https://acl.gov/ltc/costs-and-who-pays/what-is-long-term-care-insurance ("What Is Long-Term Health Insurance?"). If you have more questions about Medicaid and the partnership program in your state, check with your SHIP at shipnpr.acl.gov and consult with a lawyer well experienced with the Medicaid rules in your state.

Your support system. You may have family and friends who can provide some of your long-term care should you need it. Think about whether or not you would want their help and how much you can reasonably expect from them.

Your taxes. The benefits paid out through a long-term care policy are generally not taxed as income. Also, most policies sold today are "tax-qualified" by federal standards. This means if you itemize deductions and have unreimbursed medical expenses in excess of 10 percent of your adjusted gross income (as of 2022), you can deduct the premium cost from your federal income taxes.

Insurance providers. Some employers offer group long-term care policies or make individual policies available at discounted group rates. Many group plans don't require that you meet medical requirements to qualify, at least initially. Benefits may also be available to family members, who must pay premiums and might need to pass medical screenings. In most cases, if you leave the employer or the employer stops providing the benefit, you'll be able to retain the policy or receive a similar offering if you continue to pay the premiums.

A professional or service organization you belong to might offer group-rate long-term care insurance policies to its members. Just as with employer-sponsored coverage, study your options so you'll know what would happen if coverage were terminated or if you were to leave the organization.

Joint policies. Joint policies let you buy a single policy that covers more than one person. The policy can be used by a husband and wife, two partners, or two related adults. Typically, a total or maximum benefit applies to everyone insured under the policy. For instance, if a couple has a policy with a $100,000 maximum benefit and one person uses $40,000, the other person would have $60,000 left for his or her own services. A downside is that with such a joint policy, you run the risk of one person depleting funds that the other partner might need.

Where care is provided. You'll want a policy that covers the types of communities, programs, and services that you'll want and are available where you live. With some insurance policies, you must use services from a certified home care agency or a licensed professional; other policies allow you to hire independent or non-licensed providers or family members. Companies may place certain qualifications—such as licensure, if available in your state—or restrictions on facilities or programs used. If you move to another area, check your policy. Moving might make a difference in your coverage and the types of services available.

Benefits paid. Long-term care policies can pay different amounts for different services (such as $50 a day for home care and $100 a day for skilled nursing facility care), or they may pay one rate for any service. Most policies limit the amount of benefits you can receive, such as a specific number of years or a total dollar amount. When purchasing a policy, you select the benefit amount and duration to fit your budget and anticipated needs. "Pooled benefits" allow you to use a total dollar amount of benefits for different types of services. With this coverage option you can combine services that meet your needs.

To determine how useful a policy will be to you, compare the amount of your policy's daily benefits with the average cost of care in your area . . . and remember that you'll have to pay the difference. As the price of care increases over time, your benefit will start to erode unless you select inflation protection in your policy.

Inflation protection and automatic increases. Inflation protection is an important option to consider since many people purchase long-term care insurance decades years before receiving benefits. Indexing to inflation allows the daily benefit you choose to keep up with the rising cost of care. You can increase your benefit by a given percent (5 percent is often recommended) with either compound or simple inflation protection. If you're under age 70 when you buy long-term care insurance, it's probably better to have automatic "compound" inflation protection. This means that the amount of your daily benefit increase will be based on the higher amount of coverage at each anniversary date of the policy. "Simple" inflation protection increases your daily benefit by a fixed percentage of the original benefit amount. Typically, the simple option won't keep pace with the price of services.

In lieu of automatic increases, some policies offer "future-purchase options" or "guaranteed-purchase options." These policies often start out with more limited coverage and a corresponding lower premium. At a later, designated time, you have the option of increasing your coverage—although at a substantially increased premium. If you turn down the option several times, you may lose the ability to increase the benefit in the future.

When you'll receive benefits. Be sure you understand what must happen before you can start collecting benefits under a policy. "Benefit triggers" are the conditions that must occur before you start receiving your benefits. Most companies look to your inability to perform certain activities of daily living (ADLs) to determine when you can start to receive benefits. Generally, benefits begin when you need help with two or three ADLs, such as bathing, eating, dressing, using the toilet, walking, and being continent. I always recommend that a policy includes bathing in the list of benefit triggers because this is often the first task that becomes impossible to do alone.

Pay close attention to what the policy uses as a trigger for paying benefits if you develop a cognitive impairment, such as Alzheimer's disease. This is because a person with Alzheimer's may be physically able to perform activities but is no longer capable of doing them without help. Mental function tests are commonly substituted as benefit triggers for cognitive impairments. Ask whether you must require someone to perform the activity for you, rather than just stand by and supervise you, to trigger benefits.

Exclusions. All policies exclude coverage for some conditions. Ask the agent to review these exclusions with you. Most states have outlawed companies from requiring you to stay overnight in a hospital or nursing facility for a specific number of days before qualifying for benefits. Still, some states permit this exclusion, which could keep you from ever qualifying for a benefit. Drug and alcohol abuse, mental disorders, and self-inflicted injuries are commonly excluded. Be sure that Alzheimer's disease and other common illnesses, such as heart disease, diabetes, or certain forms of cancer, are not mentioned as reasons not to pay benefits.

Waiting or elimination period. Most policies include a waiting or elimination period before the insurance company begins to pay. This period is the number of days after you are certified as "eligible for benefits," once you can no longer perform the required number of ADLs. You can typically choose from zero up to 100 days. Carefully calculate how many days you can afford to pay on your own before coverage kicks in. (The shorter the period, the higher the price of the policy.)

When premiums are waived. Many policies allow you to stop paying your premium once you've started receiving benefits. Some companies waive premiums immediately while others waive them after a certain number of days.

Guaranteed renewable. Long-term care policies are "guaranteed renewable," which means that they cannot be canceled or terminated because of the policyholder's age, physical condition, or mental health. This guarantee ensures that your policy won't expire unless you've used up your benefits or haven't paid your premium.

Buyers' remorse. Nearly all states require insurance companies to give you 30 days to review your signed policy. During this time, you can return a policy for a full refund if you change your mind.

Still have questions or concerns? Contact the agency listed for your state at www.shiptacenter.org/.

✔ Update the beneficiaries you have listed on all your insurance policies

As you locate and record all your insurance policies, take a few minutes to review your beneficiaries and successor beneficiaries. Now is a good time to make any changes and ensure your beneficiaries' contact information is up to date. Circumstances may have changed since you initially named the beneficiaries on your policies. For example, you probably don't want to have a former spouse as a beneficiary (unless you are required to maintain a policy under a divorce decree). Your family may have changed with marriages, divorces, births, adoptions, or deaths. A beneficiary you named several years ago may now be deceased.

You can name one person, your estate (if you have a trust, see Chapter 10), multiple people, or one or more organizations as your beneficiaries. It's a good idea to name successor or secondary beneficiaries in case a primary beneficiary dies before you do. If you name multiple people or organizations, you will need to indicate the percentage that each is to receive. For example, you could name your spouse as the primary beneficiary to receive 100 percent of the policy and name your three children as secondary beneficiaries, with each receiving 33 percent if your spouse dies before you do.

INSURANCE ACTION CHECKLISTS

The checklists in Chapter 3 are set out in the following order:

- *Annuity*
- *Health Insurance: Group, Private, Medicare, and Long-Term Care*
- *Homeowners and Renters Insurance*
- *Life Insurance*
- *Umbrella Insurance*
- *Vehicle Insurance*
- *Insurance: Other Highlights*

You can download these checklists in Word or fillable PDF format at **ambar.org/AARPforms**.

Annuity

I have an annuity policy with the following companies:

Insurance company: ______________________________

Agent: ______________________________

Phone: ______________________ Fax: ______________________

Address: ______________________________

E-mail: ______________________ Website: ______________________

Policy #: ______________________________

Terms: ______________________________

Beneficiary/beneficiaries: ______________________________

Where to find the policy: ______________________________

Premium:

❑ Paid in full the amount of $__________ on (date) ______________________

❑ Paid in installments of $____________ due ______________________

  ❑ Paid by check

  ❑ Paid by autopayment from ______________________________ (account)

Insurance company: ______________________________

Agent: ______________________________

Phone: ______________________ Fax: ______________________

Address: ______________________________

E-mail: ______________________ Website: ______________________

Policy #: ______________________________

Terms: ____

Beneficiary/beneficiaries: ____

Where to find the policy: ____

Premium:

❑ Paid in full the amount of $________ on (date) ______________________

❑ Paid in installments of $__________ due ______________________

  ❑ Paid by check

  ❑ Paid by autopayment from ______________________________ (account)

Insurance company: ____

Agent: ____

Phone: ______________________ Fax: ______________________

Address: ____

E-mail: ______________________ Website: ______________________

Policy #: ____

Terms: ____

Beneficiary/beneficiaries: ____

Where to find the policy: ____

Premium:

❑ Paid in full the amount of $________ on (date) ______________________

❑ Paid in installments of $__________ due ______________________

  ❑ Paid by check

  ❑ Paid by autopayment from ______________________________ (account)

Health Insurance: Group, Private, Medicare, and Long-Term Care

I have the following types of health insurance:

- ❑ Dental
- ❑ Disability
- ❑ Health
  - ❑ Group policy through employer/union/group
  - ❑ Marketplace
  - ❑ Private health
  - ❑ Medicare Parts A and B
  - ❑ Medicare Advantage
  - ❑ Medicare Part D Prescription Insurance
  - ❑ Medicare Supplemental (Medigap)
- ❑ Travel medical
- ❑ Vision
- ❑ Other health insurance
- ❑ Long-term care

❑ I have ***dental*** insurance:

- ❑ Group policy through my employer, union, or association
- ❑ Private coverage

Where to find the policy: ____________________

Where to find the insurance card: ____________________

Insurance company: ____________________

Policy #: ____________________

Group #: ____________________

Premium:

❑ Deductions of $_________ through wages or salary

❑ Paid in installments of $_________ due ____________________________________

❑ Paid by check

❑ Paid by autopayment from __________________________________ (account)

Agent: ____

Phone: ___________________________ Fax: ______________________________

Address: ____

E-mail: __________________________ Website: ___________________________

❑ I have ***disability*** insurance:

❑ Group policy through my employer, union, or association

❑ Private coverage

Where to find the policy: ____

Where to find the insurance card: _______________________________________

Insurance company: ____

Policy #: ____

Group #: ____

Premium:

❑ Deductions of $_________ through wages or salary

❑ Paid in installments of $_________ due ____________________________________

❑ Paid by check

❑ Paid by autopayment from __________________________________ (account)

Agent: ____

Phone: ____________________ Fax: ______________________

Address: ____

E-mail: ____________________ Website: __________________

❑ I have ***group health*** insurance

Insurance company: ___________________________________

Policy #: ____

Group #: ____

Premium:

❑ Deductions of $_________ through wages or salary

❑ Paid in installments of $_________ due _________________

- ❑ Paid by check
- ❑ Paid by autopayment from ______________________ (account)

Agent: ____

Phone: ____________________ Fax: ______________________

Address: ____

E-mail: ____________________ Website: __________________

❑ I have ***Marketplace*** health coverage

Insurance company: ___________________________________

Policy #: ____

Group #: ____

Premium:

❑ Deductions of $_________ through wages or salary

❑ Paid in installments of $_________ due ____________________________________

❑ Paid by check

❑ Paid by autopayment from ____________________________________ (account)

Agent: ____

Phone: ___________________________ Fax: _______________________

Address: ____

E-mail: __________________________ Website: ____________________

❑ I have ***private*** health coverage

Insurance company: ____

Policy #: ____

Group #: ____

Premium:

❑ Deductions of $_________ through wages or salary

❑ Paid in installments of $_________ due ____________________________________

❑ Paid by check

❑ Paid by autopayment from ____________________________________ (account)

Agent: ____

Phone: ___________________________ Fax: _______________________

Address: ____

E-mail: __________________________ Website: ____________________

❑ I have the following ***Medicare*** insurance

❑ Medicare Part A

❑ No premium

❑ Monthly premium of $____________________ due ____________________

❑ Deducted from Social Security benefit

❑ Medicare Easy Pay

❑ Online with Medicare account ____

❑ Bank online bill pay through ______________________________ (account)

❑ Check

❑ Medicare Part B

❑ No premium

❑ Monthly premium of $____________________ due ____________________

❑ Deducted from Social Security benefit

❑ Medicare Easy Pay

❑ Online with Medicare account ____

❑ Bank online bill pay through ______________________________ (account)

❑ Check

❑ Medicare Advantage

Insurance company: ____

Policy #: ____

Group #: ____

Premium:

❑ Deductions of $______ through wages or salary

❑ Paid in installments of $______ due ____________________________________

❑ Paid by check

❑ Paid by autopayment from ______________________________ (account)

Agent: ____

Phone: ______________________ Fax: ______________________

Address: ____

E-mail: ______________________ Website: ______________________

❑ Medicare Part D (Prescription Insurance)

Insurance company: ____________________________________

Policy #: ____

Group #: ____

Premium:

❑ Includes IRMAA of ____________

❑ Paid in installments of $_____ due ______________________

❑ Paid by check

❑ Paid by autopayment from ______________________ (account)

Agent: ____

Phone: ______________________ Fax: ______________________

Address: ____

E-mail: ______________________ Website: ______________________

❑ Medicare Supplemental (Medigap)

I have this plan (indicate one):

Plan A Plan B Plan C Plan D Plan F Plan G Plan K Plan L Plan M Plan N

Insurance company: ____________________________________

Policy #: ____

Group #: ____

Premium:

❑ Paid in installments of $______ due ______________________________

❑ Paid by check

❑ Paid by autopayment from ______________________________ (account)

Agent: ______________________________

Phone: ______________________________ Fax: ______________________________

Address: ______________________________

E-mail: ______________________________ Website: ______________________________

❑ I have ***travel medical*** insurance

It covers (indicate all that apply):

emergency medical services hospitalization evacuation

Insurance company: ______________________________

Policy #: ______________________________

Group #: ______________________________

Premium:

❑ Paid in installments of $______ due ______________________________

❑ Paid by check

❑ Paid by autopayment from ______________________________ (account)

Agent: ______________________________

Phone: ______________________________ Fax: ______________________________

Address: ______________________________

E-mail: ______________________________ Website: ______________________________

❑ I have ***vision*** insurance

Insurance company: ____

Policy #: ____

Group #: ____

Premium:

❑ Deductions of $______ through wages or salary

❑ Paid in installments of $______ due ________________________________

❑ Paid by check

❑ Paid by autopayment from ______________________________ (account)

Agent: ____

Phone: ________________________ Fax: ___________________________

Address: ____

E-mail: ________________________ Website: _________________________

❑ I have ***other health*** insurance

Insurance company: ____

Policy #: ____

Group #: ____

Premium:

❑ Deductions of $______ through wages or salary

❑ Paid in installments of $______ due ________________________________

❑ Paid by check

❑ Paid by autopayment from ______________________________ (account)

Agent: ____

Phone: ______________________ Fax: ______________________

Address: ____

E-mail: ______________________ Website: ____________________

- ❑ I have ***long-term care*** insurance
  - ❑ Group policy through my employer, union, or association
  - ❑ Private coverage

Insurance company: ____________________________________

Policy #: ____

Group #: ____

Premium:

- ❑ Deductions of $______ through wages or salary
- ❑ Paid in installments of $______ due ____________________
  - ❑ Paid by check
  - ❑ Paid by autopayment from ____________________ (account)

Agent: ____

Phone: ______________________ Fax: ______________________

Address: ____

E-mail: ______________________ Website: ____________________

The long-term care policy has been reviewed by the following lawyer:

Name: ____

Phone: ____________________ E-mail: ________________________

Address: ____

____

The policy contains the following terms:

Triggers to begin claiming benefits

- ❑ Inability to perform _______ activities of daily living (ADLs)
- ❑ Evaluation by company's medical professionals
- ❑ Documentation by primary physician
- ❑ Moderate cognitive impairment
- ❑ Required inpatient hospital stay of _________ days
- ❑ Other: ______________________________________

Waiting period between eligibility and benefit payment of _____ days

Deductible: $____

Total days/years of coverage: ________________________________

Benefit maximum: $ _______________________________________

Daily rate: $____

Joint coverage for ________________________ and ____________________

Inflation protection: Yes No

- ❑ Compound
- ❑ Simple

Premium waiver when benefits begin: Yes No

Benefit payments are taxable income: Yes No

Nonforfeiture benefits: Yes No

Coverage includes:

❑ Home health care expenses

Licensed professional required: Yes No

Payment details: ______________________________

❑ Assisted living expenses

Certified facility required: Yes No

Payment details: ______________________________

❑ Skilled nursing facility expenses

Medicare approved facility required: Yes No

Payment details: ______________________________

❑ Compensation of family caregivers: Yes No

❑ Adult day care: Yes No

❑ Care coordination: Yes No

❑ Pooled benefits Yes No

❑ Reimbursement of home modification: Yes No

❑ State Partnership Program to qualify for Medicaid: Yes No

❑ Other coverage: ______________________________

Coverage excludes:

❑ Conditions: ______________________________

❑ Services: ______________________________

Medicare Claims Tracker

Date of service	Provider	Service (office visit, lab, etc.)	Medicare paid	Other insurance paid	Patient owes	Date paid	How paid (check, credit card)	Round trip mileage/ parking

Homeowners and Renters Insurance

Insurance company: ______________________________

Policy #: ______________________________

Agent: ______________________________

Phone: ____________________ Fax: ____________________

Address: ______________________________

E-mail: ____________________ Website: ____________________

Where to find the policy: ______________________________

Description of coverage:

____

____

Policy premium amount $______________________________

- ❑ Premium paid (indicate one): annually monthly other______________
- ❑ Paid by check
- ❑ Paid by autopayment from ______________________ (account)

Insurance company: ______________________________

Policy #: ______________________________

Agent: ______________________________

Phone: ____________________ Fax: ____________________

Address: ______________________________

E-mail: ____________________ Website: ____________________

Where to find the policy: ______________________________

Description of coverage:

____

____

Policy premium amount $______________________________

- ❑ Premium paid (indicate one): annually monthly other______________
- ❑ Paid by check
- ❑ Paid by autopayment from ________________________ (account)

Life Insurance

Insurance company: ______________________________

Type of coverage: (whole life, term, other) ______________________________

Policy #: ______________________________

Face amount: ____________ Beneficiary/beneficiaries: ______________________________

Agent: ______________________________

Phone: ______________________________ Fax: ______________________________

Address: ______________________________

E-mail: ______________________________ Website: ______________________________

Where to find the policy: ______________________________

Premium:

- ❑ Deductions of $______ through wages or salary
- ❑ Paid in installments of $______ due ______________________________
- ❑ Premium paid (indicate one): in full annually monthly other ______________
  - ❑ Paid by check
  - ❑ Paid by autopayment from ________________________ (account)

Insurance company: ______________________________

Type of coverage: (whole life, term, other) ______________________________

Policy #: ______________________________

Face amount: ____________ Beneficiary/beneficiaries: ______________________________

Agent: ______________________________

Phone: ______________________________ Fax: ______________________________

Address: ____

E-mail: __________________________ Website: ______________________

Where to find the policy: ________________________________

Premium:

- ❑ Deductions of $______ through wages or salary
- ❑ Paid in installments of $______ due ______________________
- ❑ Premium paid (indicate one): in full annually monthly other __________
  - ❑ Paid by check
  - ❑ Paid by autopayment from __________________________ (account)

Umbrella Insurance

Insurance company: ____

Policy #: ____

Group #: ____

Type of policy: ____

Where to find the policy: ____

Premium:

❑ Paid in installments of $______ due ______________________________

❑ Premium paid (indicate one): in full annually monthly other ______________

  ❑ Paid by check

  ❑ Paid by autopayment from ______________________________ (account)

Agent: ____

Phone: ______________________ Fax: ______________________

Address: ____

E-mail: ______________________ Website: ______________________

Insurance company: ____

Policy #: ____

Group #: ____

Type of policy: ____

Where to find the policy: ____

Premium:

❑ Paid in installments of $______ due ____

❑ Premium paid (indicate one): in full annually monthly other ______________

❑ Paid by check

❑ Paid by autopayment from ________________________________ (account)

Agent: ____

Phone: ____________________________ Fax: ______________________________

Address: ____

E-mail: ___________________________ Website: ___________________________

Vehicle Insurance

Vehicle: ____

Year purchased: ____________________ Purchase price: ____________________

Insurance company: ____

Agent: ____

Phone: ____________________ Fax: ____________________

Address: ____

E-mail: ____________________ Website: ____________________

Policy #: ____

Where to find the policy: ____

Premium:

❑ Paid in installments of $______ due ______________________________

❑ Premium paid (indicate one): in full annually monthly semiannually other______________________________

- ❑ Paid by check
- ❑ Paid by autopayment from ______________________________ (account)

Vehicle: ____

Year purchased: ____________________ Purchase price: ____________________

Insurance company: ____

Agent: ____

Phone: ____________________ Fax: ____________________

Address: ____

E-mail: ______________________________ Website: ______________________________

Policy #: ____

Where to find the policy: ____

Premium:

❑ Paid in installments of $______ due ____________________________________

❑ Premium paid (indicate one): in full annually monthly semiannually other______________________________________

❑ Paid by check

❑ Paid by autopayment from _______________________________________ (account)

Insurance: Other Highlights

CHAPTER 4

MY BANKING AND SAVINGS

Banks used to be pretty plain vanilla. They offered checking and savings accounts, lent money to buy homes and cars, and maybe gave you a toaster when you opened a new account. Now you can take advantage of a proliferation of services and have multiple types of accounts. In addition to a checking account and a savings account, you might have a certificate of deposit or money market account; carry a bank debit or credit card; use a financial adviser housed in the bank; rely on the automatic teller machine (ATM) to withdraw cash and transfer funds between accounts; and pay your bills online. Thanks to interstate banking, you may use different banks—both brick and mortar and online—for different types of services. However and wherever you bank, this chapter helps you track your various banking services and let your family know about your different types of accounts, where they are located, account numbers, personal identification numbers (PINs), and more.

To help you plan, I've also included a primer on the various types of banking products and the ways accounts can be titled, which determines who gets the money in your account when you pass on.

My To-Do Checklist

Done	Need to Do	
❑	❑	Review how your bank accounts are titled
❑	❑	List all banks where you do business and note their benefits and fees
❑	❑	Make sure that your accounts are FDIC insured
❑	❑	List credit unions where you do business
❑	❑	Assemble (while keeping them secure) account numbers, PINs, ATM passwords, and online banking usernames and passwords
❑	❑	Keep a record of all savings bonds
❑	❑	Let someone know where safe deposit boxes and keys are located
❑	❑	Complete the checklists for Chapter 4

✔ Review how your bank accounts are titled

How you title, or own, your bank accounts can make a big difference because it determines who can access your accounts now and who will be entitled to the money in the accounts when you die. Among the possible ways you can own bank accounts are these:

Individually: You and only you can access the money in this account. Upon your death, money remaining in this account will be distributed according to the terms of your will, or if you do not have a will, according to state law. Every state has a formula for how your assets will be distributed if you don't have a will. This law of intestacy, or descent and distribution, is explained in detail in Chapter 8.

Agency or convenience account: You can access the money in this account, but you can also designate a co-signer. A co-signer can make withdrawals but the money does not belong to the co-signer upon your death. This is the type of account people often use if they want a family member to have access to the account to help pay bills when they are out of town or in the hospital. Money remaining in this account will be distributed according to the terms of your will or, if you do not have a will, according to state law.

Joint with right of survivorship: All money in the account belongs to you and the co-owner. Upon your death, the money in the account automatically goes to the surviving co-owner. Adding a son, daughter, or any other person to your account as joint owner is the same as making a gift of all money now on deposit and any future deposits. The co-owner can write checks for any purpose and could, in fact, withdraw it to zero and head for Tahiti. For Medicaid purposes, adding a joint owner other than your spouse to an account could result in delaying your eligibility for Medicaid, as I explain in Chapter 3.

Pay on death (POD): The person you name as beneficiary has no access to money in the account while you're alive but upon your death automatically receives the balance. You can change the beneficiary, spend the money, or close the account at any time. Some people use a POD account to set aside money to pay funeral expenses.

✔ List all banks where you do business and note their benefits and fees

Commercial banks offer a wide range of services. They handle savings and checking accounts and make short- and long-term loans for personal and business use. Many also provide estate, trust, and investment services.

Checking accounts are considered **demand deposits**. In other words, as the depositor, you have the right to demand, or to withdraw, any or all your funds at any time during regular banking hours or when the ATM is open. Many financial institutions now offer interest-bearing checking accounts, but typically their interest rate is very low. In comparing bank services, note all potential fees and requirements. Banks may, for example, require a minimum balance, restrict the number of checks or withdrawals you can make in a month, or require a minimum number of direct deposits every month. You may be charged a fee when making certain transactions or using an ATM more than a certain number of times or out of the bank's network. Most banks charge stiff overdraft and/or not sufficient funds fees for each overdrawn check. They may offer overdraft protection by linking your checking account to your savings account, although some institutions will charge a fee for overdraft protection. Banks must disclose in writing the fees they charge, so read the fine print. When you list the bank accounts you now have, check out the fees and restrictions. You may want to compare with other options.

Savings accounts are another type of demand deposit. Savings accounts will probably pay you higher interest than a checking account. Depending on the bank's policies, you may have restrictions on, for instance, the number of withdrawals you can make in a month and a minimum balance.

Money market savings accounts pay a higher rate of interest than a standard savings account but may require a certain minimum balance in your account. They often include check writing and debit card privileges but may be less flexible than a regular checking account. Don't confuse this type of account at a financial institution with a money market mutual fund (discussed in Chapter 5).

Certificates of deposit are **time deposits**. Customers who use certificates of deposit (CDs) agree to leave their money in the bank for a certain period—for example, two years. During that time, withdrawals incur significant interest penalties. In return for having this long-term use of your money, banks generally pay a higher rate of interest than they do for other interest-bearing accounts.

Factors that affect the interest you can earn on your accounts include your bank's method of compounding interest and of crediting the funds you put in the account and the money you withdraw. Banks can compound interest in a variety of ways, so it pays to compare the details before opening interest-bearing checking and savings accounts or buying CDs.

✔ Make sure that your accounts are FDIC insured

Most banks insure their deposits through the Federal Deposit Insurance Corporation (FDIC). This governmental agency was established to protect people from losing their deposited assets if a bank fails. Be sure that your bank is insured by the FDIC. If so, your account could be insured up to $250,000.

FDIC insurance protects checking and savings accounts, money market deposit accounts, certificates of deposit, and IRA accounts. It does not insure any other type of investment products you might purchase through your bank, such as mutual funds. If the total amount of your deposits exceeds the maximum amount of deposit insurance, you can establish accounts in several name combinations (for example, one spouse alone, both spouses, spouse and child) or in several banks. To check the coverage limits on your accounts, use the FDIC's Electronic Deposit Insurance Estimator (EDIE) calculator at https://edie.fdic.gov/.

✔ List credit unions where you do business

Credit unions work very much like banks, although they are organized differently from banking institutions. Typically, you need to be a member of some identified group to have an account, but in turn you become a part owner of the credit union, along with all the other depositors. Credit unions offer services that encourage you to save and often provide its members loans at lower rates. They offer checking and savings accounts (although they may be called share or draft accounts), credit cards, and online banking. Federally chartered credit unions are regulated by the National Credit Union Administration. Check to make sure your credit union account is insured by the National Credit Union Share Insurance Fund (NCUSIF). Like the FDIC, the NCUSIF insures credit union accounts up to $250,000. You can find or check out a credit union at www.ncua.gov/DataApps/ResearchCU/Pages/default.aspx.

✔ Assemble (while keeping them secure) account numbers and your access PINs, ATM passwords, and online banking usernames and passwords

With today's multiple ways to do banking, we can accumulate a bewildering collection of credit, debit, and ATM cards; PINs; usernames; passwords; and security questions. These are the keys that you use to do your banking without ever entering a bank. You use them to get cash from an ATM and transfer funds, make deposits, and pay bills via online banking.

But beware: They are also the very valuable keys that others can use to raid your accounts. You need to be extraordinarily careful about lending your ATM card, keeping your PIN private, and creating your passwords. For example, don't record your PIN on a piece of paper that you carry next to your debit card. Make sure that no one is looking over your shoulder when you enter your PIN at an ATM. Change your passwords frequently and avoid something that would be obvious to a hacker, such as your mother's maiden name, birth date, or child's name. Identity thieves can easily find this information about you on the Internet, on social networking, school alumni, or genealogical sites. Using numbers, symbols, and a mix of uppercase and lowercase letters can help you build stronger passwords. For tips on creating safe passwords and more, see AARP's *My Online Privacy for Seniors* at AARP.org/techbooks.

✔ Keep a record of all savings bonds

Savings bonds have long been an easy and secure way to save. This is a good time to determine whether any bonds you may have stashed away are still a good investment. In the Savings Bonds checklist in this chapter, list each bond you are holding, the type series (E, EE, H, HH, or I), denomination, and issue date. Upon your death, your family can easily locate this potentially valuable asset.

Check whether any bonds you hold have reached maturity. Depending on what type of savings bonds you have purchased and their maturity date, they may still be earning interest, or just sitting at maturity and no longer growing. There is more than $15 billion in unredeemed bonds. The U.S. Treasury Department does not send out notices when bonds have reached maturity and stopped earning interest, but it is easy to find out. You can use the Treasury Hunt® tool on the web at www.treasurydirect.gov/indiv/tools/tools_treasuryhunt.htm to find out how much each bond is worth today. The Treasury Hunt tool lists bonds that have reached final maturity and were issued after 1974. This site will also tell you how to file claims for lost, stolen, destroyed, or undelivered bonds. While I was shredding some old papers, I stumbled across a $100 saving bond that was 15 years old. It was still earning interest, but I decided to cash it in just so I wouldn't lose it again.

The best way to cash in a paper savings bond is to take it to your local bank. You may want to consider moving your mature savings bonds to a TreasuryDirect account where the proceeds will be deposited to an electronic Certificate of Indebtedness. Find out more about how this works at Smart Exchange: https://www.treasurydirect.gov/indiv/research/indepth/smartexchangeinfo.htm.

✔ Be sure that someone knows where safe deposit boxes and keys are located

Most banks rent safe deposit boxes for a yearly fee or provide them as a free service or at a discounted cost, depending on the type of checking or savings accounts you have. Safe deposit boxes provide a place for storing valuables and documents at no or little cost. You may want to store in your safe deposit box important papers such as your marriage license, deeds to your real estate, car titles, and insurance policies. Safe deposit boxes can also protect your stock certificates, gold, silver, special jewelry and other valuables from both physical burglary and fire damage. Be sure to record what is in your safe deposit box in the Where to Find It checklist in Chapter 1.

Safe deposit boxes come with a key. When you want to store items or access items, you must use both your key and a bank key simultaneously. Neither key alone will open the box, as a safety precaution. For further protection, you must also provide your signature and identification each time you seek access to the box. Your signature will be compared to the signature that you placed on file when you first rented the box.

To protect you and the property in your box, banks restrict who can get into your box, as well as when and how they can do so. These security protections may hinder your family's need to have ready and easy access to your will or advance directives, so you won't want to keep your will and advance directives in your safe deposit box.

A safe deposit box, like a bank account, may be owned in your name only or jointly. Joint ownership gives someone else access to your box should you need to get something out of the box when you are sick or out of town. In addition, joint ownership allows the co-owner access to the box after your death.

While joint owners of a safe deposit box have access to the box, access does not mean that they own the contents of the box. Putting your diamond ring into a safe deposit box does not change the ring's owner or make a gift of the ring to the joint owner of the box. The ring will be part of your probate estate. If you have any questions about the rights of a co-owner to your box, check with your bank or your lawyer.

Most states require the bank to seal a safe deposit box upon learning of the death of an owner. They then allow a surviving co-owner or the executor to open the box in the presence of a bank or government official. An inventory of all the contents needs to be made and delivered to the probate court. This process ensures that your assets are properly reported to the court and that the applicable estate or inheritance taxes are applied to the contents of the box.

BANKING AND SAVINGS ACTION CHECKLISTS

The checklists in Chapter 4 are set out in the following order:

- *Certificates of Deposit*
- *Checking and Savings Accounts*
- *Credit Unions*
- *Safe Deposit Boxes*
- *Savings Bonds*
- *Banking and Savings: Other Highlights*

You can download these checklists in Word or fillable PDF format at **ambar.org/AARPforms**.

Certificates of Deposit

Name of institution: ______________________________

Account #: ______________________________

Initial deposit(s): $ ______________________________

Maturity date(s): ______________________________

Phone: ______________ Fax: ______________

Address: ______________________________

E-mail: ______________ Website: ______________

Online user ID: ______________________________

Online password: ______________________________

Name of institution: ______________________________

Account #: ______________________________

Initial deposit(s): $ ______________________________

Maturity date(s): ______________________________

Phone: ______________ Fax: ______________

Address: ______________________________

E-mail: ______________ Website: ______________

Online user ID: ______________________________

Online password: ______________________________

Name of institution: ____

Account #: ____

Initial deposit(s): $ ____

Maturity date(s): ____

Phone: ____________________ Fax: ____________________

Address: ____

E-mail: ____________________ Website: ____________________

Online user ID: ____

Online password: ____

Name of institution: ____

Account #: ____

Initial deposit(s): $ ____

Maturity date(s): ____

Phone: ____________________ Fax: ____________________

Address: ____

E-mail: ____________________ Website: ____________________

Online user ID: ____

Online password: ____

Checking and Savings Accounts

Name of institution: ______________________________

Phone: ____________________ Fax: ____________________

Address: ______________________________

Website:______________________________

Account #:______________________________

ATM PIN #: ______________________________

Online banking user ID: ______________________________

Online banking password: ______________________________

Name of institution: ______________________________

Phone: ____________________ Fax: ____________________

Address: ______________________________

Website:______________________________

Account #:______________________________

ATM PIN #: ______________________________

Online banking user ID: ______________________________

Online banking password: ______________________________

Name of institution: ______________________________

Phone: ______________________ Fax: ______________________

Address: ______________________________

Website:______________________________

Account #:______________________________

ATM PIN #: ______________________________

Online banking user ID: ______________________________

Online banking password: ______________________________

Name of institution: ______________________________

Phone: ______________________ Fax: ______________________

Address: ______________________________

Website:______________________________

Account #:______________________________

ATM PIN #: ______________________________

Online banking user ID: ______________________________

Online banking password: ______________________________

Credit Unions

Name of institution: ____

Phone: ______________________ Fax: ______________________

Address: ____

Website: ____

Account #: ____

ATM PIN #: ____

Online user ID: ____

Online password: ____

Name of institution: ____

Phone: ______________________ Fax: ______________________

Address: ____

Website: ____

Account #: ____

ATM PIN #: ____

Online user ID: ____

Online password: ____

Name of institution: ______________________________

Phone: ____________________ Fax: ____________________

Address: ______________________________

Website: ______________________________

Account #: ______________________________

ATM PIN #: ______________________________

Online user ID: ______________________________

Online password: ______________________________

Name of institution: ______________________________

Phone: ____________________ Fax: ____________________

Address: ______________________________

Website: ______________________________

Account #: ______________________________

ATM PIN #: ______________________________

Online user ID: ______________________________

Online password: ______________________________

Safe Deposit Boxes

Name of institution: ______________________________

Phone: ____________________ Fax: ____________________

Address: ______________________________

E-mail: ____________________ Website: ____________________

Box #: ______________________________

Where to find key: ______________________________

Box rent: $______________________________

Things I have stored in this box:

____

____

____

____

Name of institution: ______________________________

Phone: ____________________ Fax: ____________________

Address: ______________________________

E-mail: ____________________ Website: ____________________

Box #: ______________________________

Where to find key: ______________________________

Box rent: $______________________________

Things I have stored in this box:

____

____

____

____

Also record the contents of your safe deposit box in the Where to Find It checklist in Chapter 1.

Savings Bonds

I have an Individual TreasuryDirect account:

Account name: ____

Password: ____

Account #: ____

Where to find my savings bonds: ______________________________

I have the following savings bonds: ____________________________

Series	Denomination	Serial Number	Issue Date

Banking and Savings: Other Highlights

CHAPTER 5
MY INVESTMENTS

You have multiple ways you can invest for your own financial security and build up resources to leave for your family. Whether you actively follow the stock market, use online trading, rely on a financial adviser, or keep your nest egg in mutual funds, you most likely have two basic goals. One is to have enough money throughout your retirement to cover your expenses comfortably. The other is to have enough left over to take care of your loved ones.

This chapter focuses on those investments you have in addition to your checking and savings accounts and retirement savings plans. It briefly covers some of the ways you can invest your money, including stocks, bonds, and mutual funds, so you can assess whether your investments are in the right places to secure your future. This chapter can also help with your retirement savings, which are also invested in stocks, bonds, and other securities. As I explain in Chapter 6, how your retirement savings are invested depends on the plan you are using.

You can use the checklists in this chapter as a convenient place to record information about where you have investment accounts other than your retirement plans and how your family can contact your brokers or financial advisers. If you haven't done so, now might be a good time to talk with your financial adviser about whether you want to designate anyone as a trusted contact. This is an individual you authorize the firm to contact if your adviser suspects fraud or mental decline. You'll want to select this person wisely: someone you can trust to do the right thing with private and valuable information. I selected my son, who is also my financial agent under my power of attorney (see Chapter 10). In this chapter, I also show you how to identify the fees you are paying.

My To-Do Checklist

Done	Need to Do	
❑	❑	Review your investment options and check to make sure your investments are diversified and match your investment objectives
❑	❑	Pay attention to investment fees
❑	❑	Check on the background of any financial professional
❑	❑	Organize statements you receive from your brokerage firm or investment adviser
❑	❑	Complete the checklists for Chapter 5

✔ Review your investment options and check to make sure your investments are diversified and match your investment objectives

Your investment objectives will likely change depending on your age and circumstances. You'll want to check them now to make sure they are diversified and match your investment objectives. But it's not something you do just once; plan to review your investments at least annually to make sure they are the right fit for your financial security. Here I'll walk you through some of your options.

Stocks

When you own a stock, you own part of a company. Companies sell these pieces of ownership, known as shares, to raise money to finance their business. When you buy a stock, you are basically betting that the company will grow. As the company does well, your stock generally increases in value. You can earn money on your investment when either the price of the stock rises or the company shares profits by paying a dividend. If the company does poorly, you can lose some or all the money you paid for the share.

You can invest in more than 2,400 companies listed on the New York Stock Exchange. Stocks are categorized in multiple ways: by industry (auto, biotechnology), by market sector (utilities, health care), or by geography (U.S., Asian). They can also be categorized by size, as in large-capitalization, or large-cap (generally companies worth more than $5 billion), mid-cap ($1 to $5 billion), or small-cap ($250 million to $1 billion). Another way to group stocks is based on financial experts' perception of the company's basic financial health and historical performance, which includes growth stocks, value stocks, or income stocks. Knowing how a particular company's stocks are categorized helps you diversify your investments in different types of companies. Diversification reduces your risk of losing money.

Bonds

When you buy a bond, you loan money to a business or government entity. The entity commits to paying you interest at a fixed rate for the life of the loan and to return to you the value of the loan by a certain date, called the maturity date. When you invest in a bond, you take the risk that the entity may not be able to pay the interest or the principal. You also run the risk that if interest rates rise and you sell the bond, you may not get the full value. This is because other investors can buy higher rate bonds, so you have to sell yours at a lower price to attract a buyer. If you buy a ***callable*** bond, the entity has the right to pay you back before the maturity date. This is normally done when the entity can borrow at a cheaper rate.

Bonds issued by the federal government are a safe investment because they are backed by the full faith and credit of the U.S. government. This means you are guaranteed to see your original investment returned when you hold the bond to maturity. They can be easily sold, but like all bonds, their values rise and fall as interest rates change. You pay no federal income tax on the interest you earn. Treasury bills, notes, and bonds are available with maturities ranging from one to thirty years.

State and local governments also issue bonds to pay for things like roads, schools, and public safety. You pay no federal income tax on the interest, and you may not have to pay state taxes if you live in the area where the bond is issued. Because of this tax advantage, the interest rates on governmental or municipal bonds are lower than on other types of bonds.

Mutual Funds

When you buy shares of a mutual fund, you own a bit of the various stocks, bonds, or other types of investments in the fund. Buying shares of a mutual fund helps you diversify because you are spreading the risk of losing your money among many different investments. Investments within a mutual fund are chosen by a professional manager based on the fund's investment objectives. The fund's objectives, set out in a public document called a prospectus, might be to own growth stock or government bonds or invest in a particular industry, such as pharmaceuticals.

Morningstar, a company that researches and analyzes investments, tracks the performance of more than 15,000 mutual funds. These are some of the common types of mutual funds:

- Stock funds, which invest in the stocks of many companies
- Bond funds, which are a collection of bonds
- Balanced funds, which include a mix of stocks and bonds
- Life cycle, or target retirement date, funds, designed to increase the percentage of bonds in relation to stocks as the investor gets closer to retirement age
- Money market funds, which invest in short-term, low-risk loans (not to be confused with money market accounts, which I address next)

Money Market Accounts

A ***money market account*** is a type of saving account you have at a bank. Typically, the bank will pay a higher rate of interest than on regular savings accounts. You can withdraw money at any time and access the funds by making ATM withdrawals or writing checks. As with other accounts in FDIC-insured banks, your money is insured up to $250,000. You may have to maintain a minimum amount to avoid fees and be restricted on the number of withdrawals you can make in a month.

Index Funds and Exchange Traded Funds

Index funds and Exchange Traded Funds (ETF) are investment funds similar to mutual funds. They try to replicate the performance of an index, such as the Standard & Poor's 500 index, by investing in all the securities in that index. This is called passive management, which results in lower management fees than actively managed mutual funds.

As with any type of investment, you need to carefully match the fund's objectives with your own investment objectives. You also need to pay attention to the fund's fees. High fees or expense ratios can reduce your earnings, as we discuss later in this chapter.

Education Savings (529) Plans

A 529 plan is an education savings plan operated by a state government or educational institution designed to help families set aside funds for future education costs. It is named after Section 529 of the Internal Revenue Code, which created these types of savings plans. You can set up a 529 account by naming a beneficiary—such as a child or grandchild— and then contributing money that is invested by the plan's manager. Make sure you're aware of the plan's fees to manage the account, any contribution requirements, and how you can select or change the investment options within the plan.

Education savings plans can be used for elementary, secondary, and higher education in public, private, or religious schools to pay for the qualified costs of education, such as tuition, student fees, room and board (probably only on-campus housing), computers, and school-required books and supplies. In most plans, the student can attend schools either in or out of the state where the 529 plan is located. It's up to each state to set up its own program, but most states have at least one type of plan.

Your contributions to the 529 account aren't tax deductible on your federal return, but withdrawals are tax free. Most states give special tax treatment to plan contributions. You can take money out of the plan that you've contributed for other purposes, but there will be tax consequences. Most plans allow you to change the beneficiary to another family member, if the first beneficiary no longer needs the money. Money you've contributed to a 529 plan is considered a completed gift, so the money in the plan is not part of your assets upon your death. Some states, however, may consider the money you have contributed to a 529 plan in determining whether you are eligible for Medicaid. Check with an elder law attorney about the Medicaid rules in your state.

✔ Pay attention to investment fees

With any type of investment, you need to not only carefully match the fund's objectives with your own investment objectives, but you also need to pay attention to the fund's fees. High fees or expense ratios can reduce your earnings significantly.

Even seemingly small differences in expenses—say, half a percentage point a year—can make a big difference in how much wealth you accumulate over time. Here's an example from the Investor Protection Trust, a nonprofit devoted to investor education: Suppose you have $10,000 to invest for retirement, which is 30 years away. You can buy Mutual Fund ABC, which invests in stocks of big U.S. companies, or Mutual Fund XYZ, which does the same. The only difference is that fund ABC charges annual expenses of 1.5 percent per year, and fund XYZ charges 0.5 percent per year. Before expenses, the stocks in both funds return, on average, 10 percent per year. The impact of fees, though, can be dramatic. After ten years, ABC is worth $22,600, while XYZ is worth $24,700. At the end of 20 years, the difference is even more dramatic: ABC is worth $51,100, and XYZ has grown to $61,400. At retirement in 30 years, ABC has grown to $115,500, and XYZ has grown to $152,203—a $37,000 difference! Over 30 years, that 1 percent more in expenses resulted in 24 percent less value.

In my experience, most investors don't know how much they are paying in fees that are associated with all the different investment options. It's not that we're stupid; fees can be difficult to decipher, even for employers setting up 401(k) plan options. The U.S. Labor Department has been working since 2012 to make 401(k) fee disclosures more transparent, but more work needs to be done. According to *Forbes*, even when investors can find the fees buried in the fine print, they don't know if they are paying too much. In this section I walk through the different fees associated with common investments and how to find out the fees for your current or prospective investments.

Here are some of the fees typically associated with common investments. Some fees are based on actions you take; others are charged on an ongoing basis.

Mutual Funds

You will have to dig deep into the prospectus, that fine-print document you received when you sign up for a fund or a retirement savings account, to figure out the fees you are paying. They should be disclosed under "Fund Fees & Expenses" in the fund's prospectus or on the fund's website.

Expense ratio: Mutual funds charge their operating expenses as an expense ratio that is deducted from the investment return. For example, if a fund has a 0.90 percent expense ratio, for every $1,000 invested, $9 goes toward expenses. If the $1,000 has a 1 percent return, 9 cents goes toward expenses, and the investor gets 91 cents, rather than $1. This is the percentage of the fund's total assets that goes toward paying its recurring fees every year.

Sales charges, also called **purchase fees** or a **front end load**: These are commissions—ranging from 3 to 5 percent—charged at the time an investor buys mutual fund shares. For example, if you have a 5 percent sales charge when you buy a $10 share, your purchase price is $10.50. Another way to look at it is that your share is worth $9.50 because 50 cents is charged up front.

Redemption fee or **back end load:** This is the fee you pay when you sell certain mutual funds. To discourage trading, the percentage of this surrender fee typically decreases the longer you hold on to the fund. Funds with back lend loads may be 5 percent if you sell within the first year, 3 percent if you sell in the second year, and phase out over five to six years. Mutual fund redemption fees of usually 2 percent typically disappear if you hold for a certain period—generally 60 days to a year.

12b-1 fee: Mutual funds can charge a 12b-1 fee, capped at 1 percent of the amount you've invested, for marketing expenses and shareholder services. Even so-called no-load funds (those with no front end or back end loads) can levy annual 12b-1 fees.

Management fees: Management fees are deducted from the amount invested to pay the mutual fund's portfolio manager. In total, these fees typically run from 0.5 percent to 2 percent a year. (The 12b-1 fees are part of the overall management fees.)

Investment Accounts

Investment advisory fees: These are typically a percentage of the amount of money being managed. If the investment adviser charges 1 percent for every $100,000 invested, you'd pay $1,000 year in fees. The fees are debited from the account monthly or quarterly. Most advisers charge more than 1 percent, with smaller accounts being charged a higher percent, perhaps as high as 1.75 percent. Check your account agreement with the firm for this fee.

Transaction fees: Brokerage firms typically charge transaction fees of $10 to $50 per trade each time an investor places an order to buy or sell mutual funds or stocks. A $50 fee on a $5,000 trade, for example, would equal a 1 percent fee, while that same fee on a $50,000 trade would equal only 0.10 percent. Check your account agreement with the firm.

Annual account fee: Some brokerage accounts and mutual funds charge an annual account fee of $25 to $50 to cover accounting and reporting fees, or just to maintain your account, especially if your account falls below some stated amount. This fee should be stated in in your brokerage account agreement or in the fund's prospectus.

Retirement Saving Accounts and Plans

Custodian fee: IRAs may charge what they call a custodian fee of $10 to $50 a year to cover the cost of reporting to the Internal Revenue Service. Look in the IRA management company's agreement. For the fees charged by 401(k) plans, which are subtracted before your return is reported, check your account statement documents to find the amount of money you actually paid for investment expenses. In addition, most 401(k) fees are explained in your summary plan document (SPD). You can also ask your human resources or personnel department for an explanation.

Calculators to help you determine how fees impact your savings can be found at 40lkfee.com, at https://tools.finra.org/fund_analyzer, and at bankrate.com/calculators/retirement/mutual-funds-fees-calculator.aspx.

The list could go on, but this is just a sampling of some of the fees that erode your investment savings. And you may be charged more than one of these fees for on an individual investment. Take the time to investigate the fees you are paying now, wherever your money is invested, and the fees of any investment you are considering.

✔ Check on the background of any financial professional

Many different types of professionals can assist you in managing your investments, developing an investment strategy, setting up an estate plan, and making a withdrawal plan from your pension or other retirement account. Which type of professional you should consult depends on what investment help you need. Be sure to include the financial professionals you rely on in the Contacts checklist in Chapter 1.

Certified public accountants (CPAs) are licensed by a state to offer a variety of accounting services, including tax preparation, financial audits, business valuations, and succession planning for small businesses.

Enrolled agents are federally licensed tax preparers who are qualified to represent you before the Internal Revenue Service. They have passed a comprehensive IRS examination or are former IRS employees.

Estate planning lawyers can draft legal documents, including your will and power of attorney, or develop wealth transfer strategies to ensure your estate passes to your heirs in the most tax-efficient manner.

Fee-only financial advisers are paid a specific fee for each service.

Financial planners generally take a broad view of your financial affairs. They may develop a comprehensive plan to meet your investment goals or generally advise you on financial matters. They may also manage your investment portfolio.

Insurance agents can help you with your insurance needs, including health, long-term care, and life insurance as well as annuities.

Investment advisers generally focus on managing your investments. Most are paid by taking a percentage of the assets they manage for you.

Stockbrokers buy and sell stocks and bonds and are paid by commissions on the trades they make for you. Some brokers also provide financial planning services.

Before hiring any financial professional, always ask what licenses or certifications they hold, the types of services they offer, the typical clients they work with, and how they will be compensated. You should always find out in advance how and how much you are going to pay for your financial professional's services. Get in writing whether you are paying a retainer fee upfront, being charged a set fee for each service, or having a percentage deducted from any transaction.

You can often get information on professionals by asking people you know who they trust and using online resources like these:

- Attorneys: your state bar association's website
- Brokerages, brokers, and investment advisers: www.finra.org/brokercheck
- Certified Financial Planners: https://www.letsmakeaplan.org/
- Disciplinary actions taken against CPAs: www.aicpa.org/forthepublic/disciplinary actions/pages/default.aspx
- Insurance agents: https://content.naic.org/cis_consumer_information.htm
- Investment advisers: www.adviserinfo.sec.gov

✔ Organize statements you receive from your brokerage firm or investment adviser

While much investing can be done online, keeping track of your investments may still involve lots of paper. You can accumulate a small mountain of paper associated with prospectuses, proxy notices, annual reports, and monthly and quarterly statements.

I keep a 3-inch binder for my brokerage statements. To save on space, I shred the monthly statements when I get my quarterly statement, and then shred the quarterly statements when the annual summary comes in. Another way to save on paper is to request electronic statements and notices and save them to a folder on your computer. Or you can check your statements on the firm's website. I get an e-mail notice each quarter that my new statement has been posted, alerting me that it's time to review it. By organizing your investment information, you will lessen the work that your family members will have to do when they need to manage your investments.

INVESTMENTS ACTION CHECKLISTS

The checklists in Chapter 5 are set out in the following order:

- *Education Savings (529) Plans*
- *Investment Accounts*
- *Treasury Bills and Bonds*
- *Investments: Other Highlights*

You can download these checklists in Word or fillable PDF format at **ambar.org/AARPforms**.

Education Savings (529) Plans

Institution/Brokerage firm: ______________________________

Beneficiary: ______________________________

Successor owner: ______________________________

Account #: ______________________________

Phone: ______________ Fax: ______________

Address: ______________________________

E-mail: ______________ Website: ______________

Online user ID: ______________________________

Online password: ______________________________

Institution/Brokerage firm: ______________________________

Beneficiary: ______________________________

Successor owner: ______________________________

Account #: ______________________________

Phone: ______________ Fax: ______________

Address: ______________________________

E-mail: ______________ Website: ______________

Online user ID: ______________________________

Online password: ______________________________

Institution/Brokerage firm: ______________________________

Beneficiary: ______________________________

Successor owner: ______________________________

Account #: ______________________________

Phone: ______________________ Fax: ______________________

Address: ______________________________

E-mail: ______________________ Website: ______________________

Online user ID: ______________________________

Online password: ______________________________

Investment Accounts

I have the following investment accounts for my stocks, bonds, government bonds, mutual funds, and money market funds:

Institution/Brokerage firm: ______________________________

Agent or representative: ______________________________

Account #: ______________________________

Online user ID: ______________________________

Online password: ______________________________

Phone: ____________________ Fax: ____________________

Address: ______________________________

E-mail: ____________________ Website: ____________________

Institution/Brokerage firm: ______________________________

Agent or representative: ______________________________

Account #: ______________________________

Online user ID: ______________________________

Online password: ______________________________

Phone: ____________________ Fax: ____________________

Address: ______________________________

E-mail: ____________________ Website: ____________________

Institution/Brokerage firm: ______________________________

Agent or representative: ______________________________

Account #: ______________________________

Online user ID: ______________________________

Online password: ______________________________

Phone: ________________ Fax: ________________

Address: ______________________________

E-mail: ________________ Website: ________________

Institution/Brokerage firm: ______________________________

Agent or representative: ______________________________

Account #: ______________________________

Online user ID: ______________________________

Online password: ______________________________

Phone: ________________ Fax: ________________

Address: ______________________________

E-mail: ________________ Website: ________________

Treasury Bills and Bonds

I have the following Treasury Direct account:

Account name: ______________________________

Online user ID: ______________________________

Online password: ______________________________

I have the following Treasury bills or bonds funds:

Institution/Brokerage firm: ______________________________

Account #: ______________________________

Phone: ______________________ Fax: ______________________

Address: ______________________________

E-mail: ______________________ Website: ______________________

Online user ID: ______________________________

Online password: ______________________________

Institution/Brokerage firm: ______________________________

Account #: ______________________________

Phone: ______________________ Fax: ______________________

Address: ______________________________

E-mail: ______________________ Website: ______________________

Online user ID: ______________________________

Online password: ______________________________

Institution/Brokerage firm: ______________________________

Account #: ______________________________

Phone: ______________________ Fax: ______________________

Address: ______________________________

E-mail: ______________________ Website: ______________________

Online user ID: ______________________________

Online password: ______________________________

Institution/Brokerage firm: ______________________________

Account #: ______________________________

Phone: ______________________ Fax: ______________________

Address: ______________________________

E-mail: ______________________ Website: ______________________

Online user ID: ______________________________

Online password: ______________________________

Investments: Other Highlights

CHAPTER 6
MY RETIREMENT BENEFITS

Many of us receive, or will receive, income from Social Security, pensions, 401(k)s, and IRAs. Because this is the money—along with your investments, which I go over in Chapter 5—you are going to rely on for the rest of your life, you should have the pertinent information about each of these financial sources well organized. In addition, your family's eligibility for many of these benefits may depend on whether you are eligible. For example, if you have a pension or any retirement savings plans, your family may be entitled to significant benefits and financial security from those sources after your death. In this chapter, you can pull all that information together and find explanations of the various government and retirement benefits so that you and your loved ones understand the options and how to access any benefits.

Chapter 7 is devoted to those benefits that you as a veteran may be entitled to for your service to our country. You'll find information about what might be available to you now and what benefits your spouse and dependents could also receive for their support.

My To-Do Checklist

Done	Need to Do	
❑	❑	Understand Social Security benefits for you and your survivors
❑	❑	Identify all available pension benefits
❑	❑	Consider your retirement plans
❑	❑	Verify and update the beneficiary designation on pension and retirement plans
❑	❑	Complete the checklists for Chapter 6

✔ Understand Social Security benefits for you and your survivors

Social Security can be an important source of your income. According to the Social Security Administration, among older beneficiaries, 50 percent of married couples and 70 percent of unmarried persons receive half or more of their income from Social Security. Not only is it important to you in retirement, but it can also provide continuing income when your family's support is reduced or stopped because of your disability or death.

Before you or your family can receive monthly Social Security cash benefits, you must be credited for a certain amount of work under Social Security. For most benefits, you must have at least ten years of Social Security-covered employment. Just how many credits you must establish depends on your age and whether you or your family is applying for retirement, survivor, or disability benefits. You can find details on specific requirements at www.ssa.gov or at any Social Security Administration (SSA) office located throughout the country. You can find the closest office address at the SSA website at www.ssa.gov/locator.

How much Social Security retirement benefit you'll receive depends on the age at which you (and your spouse, if you are married) begin receiving benefits, whether the payments are based on your work record or your spouse's, whether you change from receiving benefits based on your spouse's record to benefits based on your earnings record, and whether your marital status changed over the years. Each year, near your birthday, Social Security sends a paper statement of your Social Security benefit. You can also go to ssa.gov/myaccount to find out how much you will receive.

Be sure you understand the best time to begin receiving retirement benefits. You can start receiving retirement checks as early as age 62 and disability checks at any age. Be aware, however, that you'll get up to 30 percent less in the monthly benefit if you begin benefits before full retirement age. If you were born between 1943 and 1954, your full retirement age is 66. If you were born after 1960, your full retirement age is 67. For those born between 1954 and 1960, the table at ssa.gov/planners/retire/agereduction.html shows how to determine your full retirement age. If you wait until age 70 to take Social Security retirement benefits, you get an additional amount—up to 30 percent more, depending on how many months after your full retirement age you start receiving benefits. Check out all the benefit calculators at www.ssa.gov/oact/anypia/index.html for more details on how your benefit amount changes based on when you start your benefits. AARP has an online tool to help you decide the best time to take Social Security at www.aarp.org/benefits-discounts/all/ss-benefits-calculator. The Consumer Financial Protection Bureau has a similar tool at www.consumerfinance.gov/consumer-tools/retirement/before-you-claim.

If you are married, you and your spouse can determine how to get the highest benefits for both of you during retirement and after one of you dies. Spousal benefits can be confusing, but here are some basics.

How much a spouse receives depends on both spouses' work history, age benefits start, and full retirement age. A married person can receive either ***spousal benefits*** based on the other spouse's earnings record (if that spouse is already receiving Social Security) or ***retirement benefits*** based on his or her own work record, whichever offers the higher benefit. A surviving spouse can receive ***survivor benefits*** based on the earnings record of the deceased spouse.

There's an important difference between the spousal benefit and the survivor benefit. The spousal benefit amount is half of the benefit the higher-earning spouse would receive at full retirement age, regardless of when the higher-earning spouse decided to begin benefits. It doesn't matter whether the higher-earning spouse begins benefits at 62, 67, or 70, as long as that spouse is getting retirement benefits. But after the higher-earning spouse dies, the surviving spouse's benefit is equal to the amount the higher-earning spouse was receiving. If the higher-earning spouse began taking retirement benefits before full retirement age, the surviving spouse will receive a significant reduction in the amount of benefits.

If the lower-earning spouse retires first, he or she can only get benefits based on his or her own earnings history. Once the higher-earning spouse retires, the lower-earning spouse can shift to the spousal benefit, if it results in a higher amount. The age at which the lower-earning spouse begins benefits will determine the amount of the spousal benefit. As of April 2016, the higher-earning spouse cannot file for retirement benefits and then suspend that benefit. This strategy formerly allowed the lower-earning spouse to begin to receive spousal benefits while the higher-earning spouse's account was continuing to grow.

If you're married, you file a joint tax return, and your combined income falls below $32,000, your Social Security benefit is not taxed at the federal level. Half is taxed if your combined income is between $32,000 and $44,000, and 85 percent of your benefit is taxed if your income exceeds $44,000. Most states do not levy income tax on Social Security benefits, including retirement havens like Arizona, the Carolinas, and Florida. Thirteen states do tax your Social Security benefits: Colorado, Connecticut, Kansas, Minnesota, Missouri, Montana, Nebraska, New Mexico, North Dakota, Rhode Island, Vermont, Utah, and West Virginia.

Social Security may also be an important source of continuing income for your family members if you are receiving or are eligible to receive retirement or disability benefits. They are eligible for benefits under the following circumstances:

- Unmarried children under 18 (or 19 if a full-time elementary or secondary school student);
- Unmarried children 18 or over who were severely disabled before age 22 and continue to be disabled;
- A spouse 62 or older who has been married to the worker for at least one year;
- A spouse under 62 if she or he is caring for a child under 16 (or disabled) who is receiving a benefit under the worker's earnings.

A divorced spouse who has been divorced at least two years can receive benefits at age 62, regardless of whether the former spouse receives them. The marriage must have lasted ten years or more; the former spouse must be at least 62 and eligible for Social Security benefits, regardless of whether he or she has retired; and the divorced spouse must not be eligible for an equal or higher benefit on his or her own—or anyone else's—Social Security record.

A number of survivor benefits may be available to your surviving family members. Your spouse, or a minor child if there is no surviving spouse, may be entitled to a one-time $255 lump sum payment. Social Security survivors insurance can provide monthly benefits, based on your earnings record, to the following:

- Your spouse can get full benefits at full retirement age, or reduced benefits as early as age 60;
- Your disabled spouse is eligible for benefits as early as age 50;
- Your spouse at any age if he or she takes care of your child who is under age 16 or disabled, and receiving Social Security benefits;
- Your unmarried children under 18, or up to age 19 if they are attending high school full time. Under certain circumstances, benefits can be paid to stepchildren, grandchildren, or adopted children;
- Your children at any age who were disabled before age 22 and remain disabled;
- Your dependent parents who are age 62 or older.

When your family members go to the Social Security office to apply for their benefits, they will need to take with them many of the documents you assembled in Chapter 1. They will need your Social Security number, your death certificate, your marriage licenses, birth certificates of eligible children, your military discharge papers, their W-2 or self-employment tax returns, and information about all your former spouses.

You can determine how much your family could receive in benefits after you die by checking your Social Security Statement. You can review your statement at any time by creating a MySocialSecurity account at www.ssa.gov/myaccount. For more comprehensive information concerning Social Security benefits, see AARP's *Social Security for Dummies* by Jonathan Peterson (available at www.aarp.org/dummies or wherever books are sold). For answers to frequently asked questions, see AARP's Social Security Resource Center at www.aarp.org/socialsecurity. Because the Social Security Act is amended from time to time, contact the nearest Social Security office for a full explanation of your rights and those of your family under the law.

✔ Identify all available pension benefits

Many public and private employees are provided pensions through their jobs. Some pensions are entirely financed by the employer; others are co-financed by the employer and the employee. Pensions are a way to accumulate tax-advantaged savings that you can tap for a steady stream of income when you are no longer working. Pensions are called ***defined benefit plans*** because you receive a specific amount of money when you retire that is defined in the terms of the pension. To calculate how much you will receive, your plan uses a formula that includes your salary history and the number of years you continued to work after you became eligible to receive pension benefits. This is called "being vested" in the pension. At the time you begin to receive your pension, you may have an opportunity to elect whether your surviving spouse will continue to receive a portion of your pension after you die.

While many employers no longer offer pensions, it's important for you to list on the Pension checklist in this chapter all places of employment where you might have become eligible (vested) for a pension. You should check with all past employers that offered pension plans during your employment to determine whether you or your survivors could receive any payments. Verify whether survivor's benefits are available and check your designation of beneficiary.

✔ Consider your retirement plans

Many public and private employers offer ***401(k) retirement plans*** that defer taxes on both the contributions you and your employer make and the plan's earnings until you withdraw funds from the plan, usually when you retire. You will have to pay a 10 percent penalty on any money you withdraw before age 59½ in addition to income taxes.

These 401(k) plans are called ***defined contribution*** plans. You make a specific dollar contribution with each paycheck to a personal plan account. The plan invests your contributions (and your employer's, if any) in mutual funds or other investments that you select from the plan's menu of investment choices. Your plan account is credited with any returns on the investment. Have a routine place to store the statements you get—whether paper or electronic—so you can track how your investment is growing.

You will also want to review any ***individual retirement arrangements (IRAs)*** you hold. The law, as of 2022, allows a person who is under age 50 and who has earned income to deposit up to $6,000 into an IRA account each year ($7,000 for people over age 50). Contributions to your ***traditional*** IRA may be wholly or partially tax deductible or nondeductible depending on whether you are also covered by a qualified pension plan or a 401(k), your tax filing status, and your income level. Traditional IRAs delay having to pay taxes on earnings from contributions until you start to withdraw funds, usually when you have reached an age where most likely your earnings have begun to decline because you will be in a lower income tax bracket. Again, tax penalties apply to early withdrawals before age 59½, except in certain circumstances. ***Roth*** IRA contributions, on the other hand, are not deductible, but withdrawals are tax free.

While you are reviewing your IRAs, you need to check on the fees you are being charged. I go over those fees in Chapter 5.

On the checklist in this chapter, list your pension, 401s, IRAs, and any other tax-deferred retirement plans you may have. These various other qualified plans also help you defer taxes. For example, if you are self-employed, you may have established one of the various qualified plans, which allows for larger, tax-deferred yearly contributions and greater benefits than does an IRA. A ***SIMPLE*** IRA is designed to make it easier for a small employer to set up a retirement savings plan for employees. Another tax-deferred retirement plan designed for self-employed people is a simplified employee pension plan, or SEP, which is a type of IRA.

Keep in mind that not all of your retirement nest egg may pass on to your heirs. Because your savings in retirement plans allow your money to grow without paying any taxes, the tax laws require you, if you are retired, to start making withdrawals, and paying taxes, if you reach 70½ before January 1, 2020—or pay a penalty. If your 70th birthday is July 1, 2019, or later, you do not have to take withdrawals until you reach age 72. If you haven't retired by the required age, you can delay withdrawals until you retire. These withdrawals are called Required Minimum Distributions (RMDs). The RMD rules apply to all employer-sponsored retirement plans, including profit-sharing plans, 401(k) plans, 403(b) plans, and 457(b) plans. The RMD rules also apply to traditional IRAs and IRA-based plans, such as SEPs, SARSEPs, and SIMPLE IRAs. The IRS provides life expectancy tables and worksheets you can use to calculate the amount of your RMD; go to irs.gov and search "RMD." The tax penalties for failing to take the correct RMDs are a stiff 50 percent of the amount owed. The Roth IRA rules are different because you have paid taxes on the money you contributed.

You can start taking withdrawals without penalty at any time after age 59½ and you can withdraw more than the required minimum amount.

If you die before age 72 or 70½, depending on your birthday, the beneficiaries of your 401(k) or IRA are subject to special tax rules. Generally, the entire amount in your account must be distributed to an individual beneficiary either within five years of your death or over the life of the beneficiary, starting no later than one year following your death. Your beneficiaries will need to use the specific IRS life expectancy tables to calculate withdrawals and taxes and seek expert and timely advice on how best to manage this inheritance.

✔ Verify and update the beneficiary designation on pension and retirement plans

Be sure to verify that you have designated beneficiaries for every retirement savings plan. Review your beneficiary designations to make sure the listing accurately reflects the people you want to receive any remaining funds in your plans.

Regardless of what type of retirement plans you participate in, you want your family to know about them. At your death, one or more of those plans may provide payments to your spouse, to minor children, to other designated beneficiaries, or to your estate. On the other hand, a plan may provide nothing at all to your survivors. The checklists in this chapter provide your family members with the information they need about any retirement assets in which you—and they—have an interest.

Information about survivor benefits and all the details that loved ones need to pay attention to when someone dies can be found in my *ABA/AARP Checklist for Family Survivors* (available at aarp.org/checklistforfamily or wherever books are sold).

RETIREMENT BENEFITS ACTION CHECKLISTS

The checklists in Chapter 6 are set out in the following order:

- *Pensions*
- *Retirement Plans*
- *Social Security Benefits*
- *Retirement Benefits: Other Highlights*

You can download these checklists in Word or fillable PDF format at **ambar.org/AARPforms**.

Pensions

Pension source/employer: ______________________

Pension ID #: ______________________

PIN #: ______________________

User ID: ______________ Password: ______________

Plan administrator: ______________________

Phone: ______________ Fax: ______________

Address: ______________________

E-mail: ______________ Website: ______________

Age vested: ______________ Age began withdrawal: ______________

Pension amount: $______________________

Account where pension distribution deposited: ______________

Beneficiaries: ______________________

____

Pension source/employer: ______________________

Pension ID #: ______________________

PIN #: ______________________

User ID: ______________ Password: ______________

Plan administrator: ______________________

Phone: ______________ Fax: ______________

Address: ____

E-mail: ____________________ Website: ____________________

Age vested: ____________________ Age began withdrawal: ________________

Pension amount: $____

Account where pension distribution deposited: ________________________

Beneficiaries: ____

____

Pension source/employer: ___________________________________

Pension ID #: ____

PIN #: ____

User ID: ____________________ Password: ____________________

Plan administrator: _______________________________________

Phone: ____________________ Fax: ________________________

Address: ____

E-mail: ____________________ Website: ____________________

Age vested: ____________________ Age began withdrawal: ________________

Pension amount: $____

Account where pension distribution deposited: ________________________

Beneficiaries: ____

____

Retirement Plans

I have the following ***individual retirement agreements*** (IRAs):

Financial institution holding my IRA: ______________________

IRA account #: ______________________

Phone: ______________ Fax: ______________

Address: ______________________

E-mail: ______________ Website: ______________

Plan amount: ______________ as of: ______________

User ID: ______________ Password: ______________

Beneficiaries: ______________________

____

Financial institution holding my IRA: ______________________

IRA account #: ______________________

Phone: ______________ Fax: ______________

Address: ______________________

E-mail: ______________ Website: ______________

Plan amount: ______________ as of: ______________

User ID: ______________ Password: ______________

Beneficiaries: ______________________

____

I have the following ***401(k) plans***:

Financial institution/Plan administrator: ______________________________

Account #: ______________________________

Phone: ______________________________ Fax: ______________________________

Address: ______________________________

E-mail: ______________________________ Website: ______________________________

Plan amount: ______________________________ as of: ______________________________

User ID: ______________________________ Password: ______________________________

Beneficiaries: ______________________________

____

I have the following ***403(b) plans***:

Financial institution/Plan administrator: ______________________________

Account #: ______________________________

Phone: ______________________________ Fax: ______________________________

Address: ______________________________

E-mail: ______________________________ Website: ______________________________

Plan amount: ______________________________ as of: ______________________________

User ID: ______________________________ Password: ______________________________

Beneficiaries: ______________________________

____

I have the following ***qualified plan*** (formerly called KEOGH):

Financial institution/Plan administrator: ______________________________

Account #: ______________________________

Phone: ______________________ Fax: ______________________

Address: ______________________________

E-mail: ______________________ Website: ______________________

Plan amount: ______________________ as of: ______________________

User ID: ______________________ Password: ______________________

Beneficiaries: ______________________________

____

I have the following ***SEP plan***:

Financial institution/Plan administrator: ______________________________

Account #: ______________________________

Phone: ______________________ Fax: ______________________

Address: ______________________________

E-mail: ______________________ Website: ______________________

Plan amount: ______________________ as of: ______________________

User ID: ______________________ Password: ______________________

Beneficiaries: ______________________________

____

I have the following ***Roth IRA***:

Financial institution/Plan administrator: ______________________________

Account #: ______________________________

Phone: ______________________________ Fax: ______________________________

Address: ______________________________

E-mail: ______________________________ Website: ______________________________

Plan amount: ______________________________ as of: ______________________________

User ID: ______________________________ Password: ______________________________

Beneficiaries: ______________________________

____

Social Security Benefits

Name on Social Security card: ______________________________

Social Security number: ______________________________

Full retirement age: ______________________________

Age retirement benefit began: ______________________________

Spouse's full retirement age: ______________________________

Type of monthly Social Security benefit (disability, retirement, widow): ______________

Monthly Social Security benefit: $ ______________________________

Estimate of amount my surviving dependents would receive: $______________________

Social Security benefit is deposited at (financial institution): ______________________

Retirement Benefits: Other Highlights

CHAPTER 7

MY VETERANS BENEFITS

If you have served in the United States armed forces, you and your family members may be entitled to benefits that can provide financial security and valuable services in recognition of your service to our country. As you might expect from your active duty military service, there are many details you need to know and regulations you have to follow to gain some of these benefits. I've provided you with a summary of some of them so you are aware of the range of services you could receive. The VA website at www.va.gov is a good place to start for greater details about each of the programs.

My To-Do Checklist

Done	Need to Do	
❑	❑	Make sure you have the documentation necessary to apply for benefits
❑	❑	Apply for any benefit you are currently eligible for
❑	❑	Review and select the burial benefits you prefer
❑	❑	Complete the checklists in Chapter 7

✔ Make sure you have the documentation necessary to apply for benefits

The U.S. Department of Veterans Affairs (VA) is charged with administering benefits available to people who have served on active duty in the U.S. military service. The available benefits depend upon your length of service, the era during which your service was performed, whether you are disabled, whether the disability was caused by active service, and many other criteria.

You will need to have documentation of your military service to apply for any benefits available to you or to your family. You can get a copy of your service record (DD-214) at the National Archives' "Request Military Records" website at www.archives.gov/veterans/military-service-records. You can request your own military records, including medical records, by going online at eVetRecs, https://www.archives.gov/veterans/military-service-records/evetrecs-help.html. You need to include the complete name you used while in the service, service number, Social Security number, branch of service, dates of service, and date and place of birth. You must sign and date the request and fax it to the National Personnel Record Center (NPRC) at 314-801-9195 or mail it to the NPRC, Military Personnel Records, 1 Archives Drive, St. Louis, MO 63138. Your next of kin may request military records using eVetRecs or by written application using Standard Form 180 and providing proof of death (death certificate and letter from a funeral home or published obituary). You may need a copy of your marriage license, birth certificate, and children's birth certificates or adoption papers to apply for certain benefits. Make sure you have recorded where you have these documents on the Where to Find It checklist in Chapter 1.

✔ Apply for any benefits you are currently eligible for

Under certain circumstances, the following benefits (and many more) *may* be available to you now if you are a veteran:

- Pensions for disability caused by service-connected injury or disease
- Pensions for certain nonservice-connected disabilities
- Automobile allowance for service-connected loss or permanent loss of the use of one or both hands or feet
- Hospitalization benefits
- Help paying for the assistance of another in your home
- Alcohol and drug dependence treatment
- Nursing home care
- Outpatient medical treatment
- Prosthetic appliances
- Vocational rehabilitation and counseling
- Loan guaranty benefits
- Insurance
- Federal civil service preference

✔ Review and select the burial benefits you prefer

Many other services and benefits are available to your family following your death if you are an eligible veteran:

Burial flag. A U.S. flag may be provided to drape over your casket if you are an eligible veteran. After the funeral service, the flag may be given to your next of kin or close friend or associate. Flags are issued at any VA office and most local post offices. A Presidential Memorial Certificate is also available at no cost to your family.

Burial in national cemeteries. Burial in a national cemetery is open to all members of the U.S. Armed Forces and veterans having met minimum active service duty requirements and having been discharged under conditions other than dishonorable. Your spouse, widow or widower, minor children, and, under certain conditions, unmarried adult children are also eligible for burial in a national cemetery. An eligible spouse may be buried in a national cemetery, even if he or she predeceases you. In most cases, one gravesite is provided for the burial of all eligible family members and a single headstone or marker is provided. When both you and your spouse are veterans, you can request two gravesites and two headstones or markers. Certain members of the Armed Forces reserve components may also be eligible for burial, depending on the space available. There is no charge for the grave plot, for its opening and closing, a grave liner, or for perpetual care.

Headstones or markers. The VA will furnish a government headstone or marker to be placed at your grave at any cemetery around the world. Even if the grave was previously marked, your family can obtain a government headstone. This service is provided for eligible veterans whether they are buried in a national cemetery or elsewhere. A headstone or marker is automatically furnished if burial is in a national cemetery. Otherwise, your family must apply to the VA. The VA will ship the headstone or marker, without charge, to the person or firm designated on the application. The VA will also furnish, on request, a service medallion to place on an existing headstone or marker that indicates that the person was a veteran. Your family must pay the cost of setting the headstone or marker or attaching the medallion.

Military honors. By law, every eligible veteran may receive a military funeral honors ceremony, to include folding and presenting the U.S. burial flag and the playing of Taps. A military funeral honors detail consists of two or more uniformed military persons, with at least one being a member of your branch of the Armed Forces.

The Department of Defense program "Honoring Those Who Served" calls for funeral directors to request military funeral honors on behalf of your family. Veterans' organizations may assist in providing military funeral honors. In support of this program, VA national cemetery staff can help coordinate military funeral honors either at a national or private cemetery. For more information, go to www.military.com/benefits/burial-and-memorial/military-funeral-honors.html.

Reimbursement of burial expenses. The VA is authorized to pay an allowance toward your funeral and burial expenses if you are an eligible veteran. If yours was a service-related death, the VA will pay up to $2,000 toward burial expenses. If you are to be buried in a VA national cemetery, some or all of the cost of transporting your body to the cemetery may be reimbursed. For a nonservice-related death, the VA will pay up to $300 toward burial and funeral expenses and a $300 plot-interment allowance. If your death happens while you are in a VA hospital or under VA contracted nursing home care, some or all of the costs for transporting your remains may be reimbursed.

Dependency and Indemnity Compensation (DIC). DIC payments may be authorized for your spouse, unmarried children, and low-income parents if you die during active duty or if your death is service connected. The amount of the basic benefit is determined by your military pay grade. Payments are also made for children under age 18 or up to age 23 who are attending school.

Nonservice-connected death pension. Your surviving spouse and unmarried children under age 18 or up to age 23 who are attending school may be eligible for a pension if their income does not exceed certain limits.

Education for spouses, widows, widowers, sons, and daughters. If you are completely disabled or die as a result of your military service, the VA will generally (but with some exceptions) pay to help educate your spouse, widow or widower, and each son and daughter beyond the secondary school level, including college, graduate school, technical and vocational schools, apprenticeships, and on-the-job training programs. Education loans are also available through the VA.

VETERANS BENEFITS ACTION CHECKLISTS

The checklists in Chapter 7 are set out in the following order:

- *Veterans Benefits for Me and My Caregivers*
- *Veterans Benefits upon My Death*
- *Veterans Benefits: Other Highlights*

You can download these checklists in Word or fillable PDF format at **ambar.org/AARPforms**.

Veterans Benefits for Me and My Caregivers

Name served under: ____
First *Middle* *Last*

Military service number (DD-214): ______________________________

Entered active service on ____________________________________

Separated from active service on ______________________________

Service post-9/11: Yes No

Type of discharge: ____

Branch: ____

Grade or rank: ____

National Guard: ____

Reserves: ____

VA Medical Center or clinic I use: ______________________________

Address: ____

Phone: ____

E-mail: ____

As a veteran, I am eligible or I will investigate eligibility for the following VA benefits.

Now Receiving	Will Investigate	
❑	❑	Alcohol and drug dependence treatment
❑	❑	Automobile allowance for service-connected loss or permanent loss of the use of one or both hands or feet
❑	❑	Dental care
❑	❑	Federal civil service preference
❑	❑	Help paying for the assistance of another in your home

❑	❑	Hospitalization benefits
❑	❑	Insurance
❑	❑	Loan guaranty benefits
❑	❑	Nursing home care
❑	❑	Outpatient medical treatment
❑	❑	Pension for disability caused by service-connected injury or disease
❑	❑	Pension for certain nonservice-connected disabilities
❑	❑	Prosthetic appliances
❑	❑	Vocational rehabilitation and counseling

As a disabled veteran, my caregivers and I are eligible or will investigate eligibility for the following VA benefits:

Now Receiving	Will Investigate	
❑	❑	Caregiver training
❑	❑	Case manager
❑	❑	CHAMPVA health insurance
❑	❑	Financial stipend
❑	❑	Fitness classes
❑	❑	Housing support
❑	❑	Legal guidance
❑	❑	Loans
❑	❑	Mental health services
❑	❑	Patient advocate
❑	❑	Recreational activities
❑	❑	Respite care
❑	❑	Spiritual counseling
❑	❑	Stress-relief sessions
❑	❑	Support groups
❑	❑	Travel expenses

Veterans Benefits upon My Death

Upon my death, I wish to receive the following benefits:

❑ Burial flag

❑ Burial in a national cemetery

❑ Government headstone or marker

❑ Headstone ❑ Marker

Words on headstone/marker: ______________________________

❑ Military honors

❑ Service medallion for headstone/marker

❑ Reimbursement of burial expenses

❑ Dependency and Indemnity Compensation

❑ Nonservice-connected death pension

❑ Education for spouses, widows, widowers, sons, and daughters

Veterans Benefits: Other Highlights

CHAPTER 8
MY REAL ESTATE

Your home is most likely the most valuable real estate you own. Your real estate can also include commercial property where you earn income, investment property that you rent out or plan to sell for a profit, a condominium where you own specific space, a timeshare where you have the right to access a unit of the property for a limited time, and even a burial plot.

What kind of real estate you have can determine what you can and can't do with the property. How your real estate is titled, or owned, too, makes a big difference in how ownership to that piece of property is transferred at your death and who will become the next owner. That's why, in this chapter, you have an opportunity to take stock of all your real estate and go over the ways it is, or can be, owned.

My To-Do Checklist

Done	Need to Do	
❑	❑	Assemble copies of the deeds or ownership documentation to all real estate
❑	❑	Review how your property is titled
❑	❑	Discuss your real estate ownership and taxes with a tax adviser or estate planner
❑	❑	Determine if your property qualifies for tax relief
❑	❑	Consolidate all investment and commercial property records
❑	❑	Know the details of your timeshare contract
❑	❑	Complete the checklists for Chapter 8

✔ Assemble copies of the deeds to all real estate

You can tell how you own property by looking at the documents you received at the time you acquired the property. Typically, that is called a deed. If you own a condo, you should have a copy of the master deed or declaration, which describes the space that you own, the common areas, and any restrictions on how you can use or modify your unit or the common areas. You should also have a copy of your condominium association documents: the bylaws and/or rules that further set out how the condominium is to be managed, pet restrictions, paint color choices, and how monthly unit fees are assessed, among other details. For much more information about condominium ownership, get my AARP/ABA book with co-author Lawrence Frolik, *Wise Moves: Where to Live, What to Consider, and Whether to Stay or Go*.

If you do not have a copy of any deeds, you can get a copy from the clerk of the land records in the county where the property is located. Many counties have online systems where you can search and download these documents. If you own a burial plot, you should have a deed or other documentation of ownership. You will want to keep copies of each deed in your safe deposit box. Be sure to note the location in the Where to Find It checklist in Chapter 1.

✔ Review how your property is titled

There are many ways you can own, or hold title to, real estate. How you hold title has a significant impact on what you can do now with your property and how it will be distributed at your death.

Take, for example, all the different ways you can own your home. I go into more detail on these below.

- You can own it in your own name.
- You can own it jointly with others.
- You can give away or sell ownership to someone else and keep the right to live in your home for as long as you live.
- You can own the space where you live but not the building.
- You can own the right to have access to a part of the space for a limited time.
- You can put your property into your own trust, which would then own it.

Your deed will set out how you own the property.

Be aware that instructions in your will about who is to inherit your property do not affect what you have said in a deed about who you want to inherit that property. The deed rules over the will.

Individual Ownership

You can own real property ***individually*** in your own name. This means that you alone have the right to sell it, rent it, mortgage it, use it in any legal way, and transfer it by will. You need to state in your will who you want to inherit this property. If you do not have a will, your state's ***intestacy*** law—setting up a priority of inheritance—will determine who gets it. To a degree, state intestacy laws try to anticipate who the typical person would want to inherit his or her property if the property owner had gotten around to writing a will. You should check to see what your state's priority scheme is, but typically real estate would first go to a spouse, and if no spouse then to children, and if no children then to parents, then to siblings, and so forth, moving out the multiple branches of the family tree to the closest living next of kin. Most intestacy laws also include rules of what to do when there are branches in the family tree such as deceased children with living children or multiple marriages. Only if no next of kin can be located does the state get your property, called ***escheat*** to the state.

Joint Ownership with Right of Survivorship

Joint owners with right of survivorship have equal ownership and rights to use and enjoy the property. When one of the joint owners dies, the surviving owner or owners automatically continue to own the property. The last surviving owner ends up as the sole owner of the property. This last owner can then leave that property by will to anyone he or she wants, or it will be distributed through intestacy rules. All joint owners must agree to sell or mortgage the property. For couples who are not married, this type of property ownership ensures that the surviving partner will automatically inherit the property. Joint owners don't have to be spouses. If they are, some states call this type of ownership ***tenants by the entireties***.

Joint ownership with right of survivorship is typically the way that spouses own their home because it is a convenient way to avoid the need to probate that property when the first spouse dies. A joint owner automatically inherits any jointly owned property upon your death. This can be one of the useful ways to pass property on to another without the delay of probate.

Adding a child to a deed as a joint owner: On the other hand, I've seen time and time again how adding a child to a deed because the parent wants the child to inherit a home can be fraught with negative consequences, both to the parent and child. Say you add your child to your deed as joint owner with right of survivorship. You cannot sell your home, take out a home equity loan, or get a mortgage without your child's consent. You will not be able to get a reverse mortgage unless you and your child are both over age 62. If your child is sued, gets a divorce, or goes into bankruptcy, your jointly owned home will be involved in those legal entanglements.

By adding a child to your deed as a joint owner, you are making a gift of the value of the home, which has tax and Medicaid complications. You may need to declare the gift to the IRS by preparing gift-tax returns. Refer to IRS Publication 559 at www.irs.gov/forms-pubs/about-publication-559 for more details or consult with your lawyer. Once both you and your child understand the different tax consequences between "gifting" it now and waiting until later, you may choose the latter.

One difference between a child getting the house now or waiting until your death is due to a tax rule called ***stepped-up basis***. When children inherit an asset, they are not taxed on the appreciation or increase in value that took place before they got the assets. Stepped-up basis means that a child who inherits the house would owe less in capital gains taxes when he or she later sells the house than a child who became a joint owner years earlier would owe. When you make a gift of your home by adding your child as a joint owner, your child gets the same basis as you had at the time you make the gift.

Here's how the calculation works: Say you purchased your home for $250,000 many years ago. It increased in value to $500,000 at your death. If your son ***inherited*** the home and later sells it for $600,000, he would have a basis of $500,000 and a capital gain of only $100,000. If you ***gifted*** your son the house before your death, each of you would have a basis of $125,000, half of the original basis of $250,000. As joint owner with right of survivorship, he inherits the other half of the house and your basis. This makes your son's basis $125,000 from the earlier gift plus your $250,000 basis he inherited (half of the $500,000 value at date of death) for a total basis of $375,000. If he sells at $600,000, he would have a gain of $225,000. At a 15 percent capital gains rate, the difference in tax liability is double—$15,000 versus $33,750. The homeowner exclusion of gain does not apply because your child did not live in the house.

Gifting joint ownership of your home may also prevent or delay you from being eligible for Medicaid if you need to go into a nursing home. I go into eligibility for Medicaid in Chapter 3. Note: Tax laws and Medicaid eligibility rules frequently change and vary from state to state. Check with your financial adviser and a lawyer experienced with your state's Medicaid rules before making any gift.

Common Ownership

Ownership in common (called tenants in common) is the other primary way to own real estate with someone else. The key difference between joint ownership and common ownership is what happens to the share of ownership when a common owner dies. Unlike joint ownership with right of survivorship, the surviving common owner does not inherit any greater interest or share in the property. The common owner's share passes to the decedent's estate. Siblings who together own property, such as a beach house, may want to consider ownership in common so that the siblings' interests will pass down to their own children, rather than to the sibling or nieces and nephews. For example, Juanita and Louise as sisters share equal ownership in common of a lake cabin where their families frequently spend summers. Each sister has a will that states that when she dies, her property passes to her own children. When Juanita dies, Louise still owns half of the property, along with Juanita's kids, who own the other half.

Community Property

For spouses in nine states (Arizona, California, Idaho, Louisiana, Nevada, New Mexico, Texas, Washington, and Wisconsin), all property acquired during the marriage automatically becomes community property. The laws vary in each of these states, but the basic theory is that each spouse acquires an equal interest in the real estate. When one spouse dies, only half the marital property is inheritable since the surviving spouse already owns half of the marital property. Each spouse has the right to assign by will the ownership of his or her portion of the community property. Property that either spouse brought into the marriage or inherits is considered separate property.

Trust Property

Another way to title property is to have it held in trust. You as grantor can create a trust and deed the selected real estate into the trust. Although as grantor you no longer "own" the property (your trust does), you determine who as trustee is to manage that property (it could be yourself, if you wish) and when and how the trustee is to transfer that property to the beneficiaries. The beneficiary of a trust is the person who receives the benefit of the trust. This could be you during your lifetime and those you name as beneficiaries upon your death. When and how assets in the trust are distributed to the beneficiary depends on the language in the trust document, rather than your will.

You can read more about trusts in Chapter 10.

Rental Property

As a renter, you don't own where you call "home," but you still have legal rights while you live there. You could rent an apartment, have a unit in an assisted living community, or stay in a room in a skilled nursing facility. You could also have a rental contract with a continuing care retirement community (CCRC), where you move from independent living to higher levels of services and care as your medical needs change, while staying within the same campus or residential community.

Wherever you rent your home, your rights and obligations are spelled out in the rental contract, including how long you can stay, how much you pay for rent and fees, what services you'll get, and what you need to do when you move out. You'll likely want a lawyer to review the contract, especially for CCRCs, which can be extremely complicated and have intricate fee structures. For much more information about the different housing options and their advantages and disadvantages, get my ABA/AARP book with co-author Lawrence Frolik, *Wise Moves: Where to Live, What to Consider, and Whether to Stay or Go*.

Life Estate

By creating a life estate, you transfer the ownership of your home to another person but reserve the right to continue to live in the home until you die. Upon your death, the other person automatically gets the right to take possession. A life estate is one way to create income; you basically sell your house but continue to live in it. Let's say you're an 80-year-old widow and own a house worth $300,000, but you need more money to live on. You can sell what's called a "remainder" interest in your house to a child for, say, $150,000. You now have $150,000 to cover your expenses and can live in the house until you die. At that point, your child (the "remainder person") takes possession and ownership of the house. Your child gets a house worth $300,000 while helping you financially.

Life estates are governed by state law, but almost all states require the life estate holder, not the remainder person, to pay for property taxes, insurance, and ordinary repair and maintenance of the property. The remainder person has the right to sell the remainder while the life estate holder is still alive, although few potential buyers would be interested because of the uncertainty of when they could take possession. If, however, the life tenant and the remainder person agree, together they can combine their ownerships and sell the house outright. They need to agree on how to split the sale proceeds before they sell the house.

✔ Discuss your real estate ownership and taxes with a tax adviser or estate planner

As you take inventory of your real estate and how you own it, you might find that you have different needs or plans than when you first acquired and titled it. Your personal circumstances, births of children and grandchildren, deaths of a spouse or other family members, employment status, and housing needs are just a few of the reasons you may want to take a hard look at whether you need to reconsider how you own your real estate. Before making changes to how you own any real property, however, you'll want to get sound advice from a professional about any tax, public benefits, or inheritance implications.

✔ Determine if your property qualifies for tax relief

Depending on where you live, you may be eligible for property tax relief on your residence. Most states or counties offer some reduction in taxes based on the homeowner's age, income, disability, or military status. Eligibility for these programs, which I go into here, varies. Some are based solely on age, while others have an income test to qualify. To learn about tax relief policies available in your state, visit the Lincoln Institute of Land Policy website at www.lincolninst.edu/publications/articles/how-do-states-spell-relief.

Tax Deferral

As the name suggests, a property tax deferral delays when the tax must be paid—but it doesn't reduce the amount owed. Some states pay the property taxes to the local taxing authority, such as a school district. The state then expects repayment from the homeowner at some later date. Most such programs have a minimum age requirement. For example, the state of Washington has a minimum eligibility of age 60. Many states also have a maximum income cap. The deferral may or may not include the annual interest that accumulates over the years that the taxes are deferred. The taxing authority, or the state if it pays the taxes on behalf of the property owner, places a ***lien***, an IOU, on the house in the amount of the unpaid taxes. When the house is sold or the homeowner dies, the taxes must be paid along with any accumulated interest. The amount in taxes that can be deferred depends on the home's value, either the assessed value for property tax purposes or the actual market value. If the payment of property taxes seriously reduces your quality of life or is forcing you to sell, consider investigating the option of property tax deferral. Doing so may literally save your house.

Homestead Exemptions

In some states, homestead exemptions are used to reduce the property tax burden for some older homeowners. The exemptions provide for a reduction in the assessed value of the home, which reduces the property tax. The exemptions may be a fixed dollar reduction, such as $20,000, or a percentage reduction, usually with a dollar cap on the amount.

States differ on which property tax is reduced. Some states apply the reduction to all property taxes, such as the county, the locality, and the local school district. Other states limit the exemption to a specified tax, such as the local school district property tax.

Eligibility requirements vary from state to state. Some limit the exemption to those of a minimum age, such as 60 or 65. Some states also impose an income limit. In a few states, where there is only an age requirement, the exemption is automatic. Other states require the homeowner to apply for the exemption.

Circuit Breakers

Some states and a few localities provide property tax relief through state-financed payments to localities or school districts that take the place of the homeowner paying the property tax. The state steps in to pay enough of the taxes to reduce the tax burden on the homeowner to a manageable level. The state payment is called a "circuit breaker" because, like an electric circuit breaker, the state payment protects the homeowner against an "overload" of property taxes. Typically, the state pays some portion of the property taxes of homeowners who meet minimum age requirements and whose income is below a designated amount. The lower the income of the homeowner, the greater share of the taxes paid by the state. Other states provide a set amount of tax relief to older homeowners who meet the state income requirements. There is typically no requirement that the homeowner ever repay the property taxes paid by the state.

Property Tax Freezes

Some states bar or limit any increase in property taxes for eligible older homeowners. The tax is frozen as of the year the homeowner becomes eligible for the program. As an alternative, a few states and some localities freeze the assessed value of the home. The property tax may still increase if the taxing entity raises the tax rate, but the homeowner is at least protected against an increase in property taxes because of a rise in the property's market value. A freeze in the assessment value can be quite helpful for homeowners who live in an area that is subject to gentrification or rapidly rising home prices.

Abatement of Tax Increase

A major home improvement, such as renovating a kitchen or adding a garage, can result in an increase in the home's value and possibly in its assessed value. That, in turn, increases the property tax. Some local taxing authorities may have a law or ordinance that bars certain improvements from causing an increased assessment in the home's value for qualified homeowners. This is commonly referred to as a tax abatement.

The abatement of an assessment increase is usually available to all homeowners. Most programs do not have an age or income requirement. Not all improvements qualify. For example, the addition of an in-ground swimming pool may still result in an increase in assessed value. A few abatement programs may be limited to designated areas, such as a recognized historical district. To qualify, you'll probably have to apply for the abatement.

To find out if you are eligible for any form of tax relief, contact the local office where you pay taxes, your state department of revenue or taxation, or your local area agency on aging.

✔ Consolidate all investment and commercial property records

You may have a second home where you spend part of the year, land that you inherited and share with other relatives, investment property that you rent out, or a farm operation that you run. As with any income-producing asset, you should maintain detailed records relating to the management of your investment or farm property. In addition to the deed, these records could include business plans, land or equipment leases, rental income, easements, assessments, insurance policies, tax records, accounts payable, and inventory of all equipment. Keeping these documents organized will help you manage your properties and, should something happen to you, help someone who might need to take over management of the property.

✔ Understand your timeshare contract

A timeshare is a way to own the right to use property, rather than direct ownership of the property. With most timeshares, multiple people have the right to use the same property, with each having a specific period of time when they have exclusive use of the property. You may purchase a specific week in a specific unit or be able to negotiate a rotating time schedule or trade your share for use of multiple properties. Companies can have timeshares around the world that you can choose from. There are many variations on the timeshare concept, but this brief description and these terms may help you better understand how your timeshare works.

There is the ***unit timeshare,*** where you purchase a specific unit at a specific resort. You own the unit. You and the other unit owners together own the resort property. You share in the use and the cost of maintaining the common grounds. This is a real estate transaction for real property just like purchasing any other real estate. You have a deed to a timeshare estate, which you can rent, sell, exchange, or pass on to your family. You pay a purchase price plus an annual maintenance fee. You are a member of a homeowners association that elects officers, manages expenses for the upkeep of the property, and probably hires a management company.

The other main type of timeshare usage is an ***interval plan***, sometimes called a vacation club. Under this arrangement, you purchase the right to use space in the resort for some set time determined by your right-to-use contract. This contract treats the timeshare as personal property, not real property; instead of holding a deed to a piece of property, you have a contract that lets you use a piece of the property. The contract can be a ***fixed time*** option, where you have the use of a fixed unit for a specific week each year for the rest of your life. Or it could be a ***floating time*** option, where you have the right to use any available unit in the resort for any week on a first-come, first-served basis. You might also have biennial ownership, accessing the property every other year, as an "odd" or "even" year user.

A variation of the interval plan is the points-based system. You buy "points" that give you the right to use any available unit in the resort's affiliated properties for a period of time that is referred to as an interval. The number of points needed to use a unit depends on how long you stay, when you stay, and where the resort is located.

Your deed or contract explains your current rights to use your timeshare and what happens to it on your death. Be sure to note the location of your deed or contract, along with contact information for the property management company and any reservations or interval points you have with the exchange company.

REAL ESTATE ACTION CHECKLISTS

The checklists in Chapter 8 are set out in the following order:

- *Business Property*
- *Condominium*
- *Investment Property*
- *Primary Residence*
- *Rental Residence*
- *Secondary Residence*
- *Timeshare*
- *Trust*
- *Real Estate: Other Highlights*

You can download these checklists in Word or fillable PDF format at **ambar.org/AARPforms.**

Business Property

Property address: ____

My ownership interest:

- ❑ Sole
- ❑ Community property
- ❑ Joint with right of survivorship
- ❑ Tenant in common
- ❑ In trust

Co-owner(s): ____

____

Purchase price: ____

I owe money on the property as follows:

Financial institution/Loan servicer: ______________________________

Phone: ____________________ Fax: ____________________

Address: ____

E-mail: ____________________ Website: ____________________

Balance due ____________________ as of ____________________ (date)

Monthly payment: ____

Property address: ______________________________

My ownership interest:

- ❑ Sole
- ❑ Community property
- ❑ Joint with right of survivorship
- ❑ Tenant in common
- ❑ In trust

Co-owner(s): ______________________________

____

Purchase price: ______________________________

I owe money on the property as follows:

Financial institution/Loan servicer: ______________________________

Phone: ______________________ Fax: ______________________

Address: ______________________________

E-mail: ______________________ Website: ______________________

Balance due ______________________ as of ______________________ (date)

Monthly payment: ______________________________

Condominium

Property address: ______________________________

Condominium association contact:

Name: ______________________________

Phone: ______________ Fax: ______________

Address: ______________________________

E-mail: ______________________________

Monthly condominium association dues: ______________________________

Purchase price: ______________________________

I owe money on the condominium as follows:

Financial institution/Loan servicer: ______________________________

Phone: ______________ Fax: ______________

Address: ______________________________

E-mail: ______________ Website: ______________

Type of mortgage: ______________________________

Balance due: ______________ as of ______________ (date)

Monthly payment: ______________________________

Investment Property

Property address: ______________________________

My ownership interest:

- ❑ Sole
- ❑ Community property
- ❑ Joint with right of survivorship
- ❑ Tenant in common
- ❑ In trust
- ❑ Life estate

Co-owner(s): ______________________________

____

Purchase price: ______________________________

I owe money on the real estate as follows:

Financial institution/Loan servicer: ______________________________

Phone: ______________ Fax: ______________

Address: ______________________________

E-mail: ______________ Website: ______________

Type of mortgage: ______________________________

Balance due: ______________ as of ______________ (date)

Monthly payment: ______________________________

Primary Residence

Property address: ______________________________

My ownership interest:

- ❑ Sole
- ❑ Community property
- ❑ Joint with right of survivorship
- ❑ Tenant in common
- ❑ In trust
- ❑ Life estate

Co-owner(s): ______________________________

____

Purchase price: ______________________________

I owe money on my residence as follows:

Financial institution/Loan servicer: ______________________________

Phone: ______________________ Fax: ______________________

Address: ______________________________

E-mail: ______________________ Website: ______________________

Type of mortgage: ______________________________

Balance due: ____________________ as of ____________________ (date)

Monthly payment: ______________________________

Rental Residence

Property address: ______________________________

Unit: ______________________________

Property manager:

Name: ______________________________

Phone: ______________________ Fax: ______________________

Address: ______________________________

E-mail: ______________________ Website: ______________________

Rental period: ______________________________

Monthly payments: ______________________________

Additional payments for services: ______________________________

Secondary Residence

Property address: ____

My ownership interest:

- ❑ Sole
- ❑ Community property
- ❑ Joint with right of survivorship
- ❑ Tenant in common
- ❑ In trust
- ❑ Life estate

Co-owner(s): ____

____

Purchase price: ____

I owe money on my secondary residence as follows:

Financial institution/Mortgage servicer: ______________________________

Phone: ______________________ Fax: ______________________

Address: ____

E-mail: ______________________ Website: ______________________

Type of mortgage: ____

Balance due: ____________________ as of ____________________ (date)

Monthly payment: ____

Timeshare

Timeshare management company: ___________________________________

Representative: ___________________________________

Phone: ______________________ Fax: ______________________

Address: ___________________________________

E-mail: ______________________ Website: ______________________

Type share: ______________________ Purchase price: ______________________

Interval exchange company contact: ___________________________________

Phone: ______________________ Fax: ______________________

Address: ___________________________________

E-mail: ______________________ Website: ______________________

I owe money on the timeshare as follows:

Financial institution/Mortgage servicer: ___________________________________

Phone: ______________________ Fax: ______________________

Address: ___________________________________

E-mail: ______________________ Website: ______________________

Type of mortgage: ___________________________________

Balance due: ______________________ as of ______________________ (date)

Monthly payment: ___________________________________

Annual maintenance fee: $ ____________________

Due date: ____________________

Due to: ____________________

Name: ____________________

Phone: ____________________ Fax: ____________________

Address: ____________________

E-mail: ____________________

Trust

I am the grantor of the following property held in trust:

Property address: ______________________________

Grantor: ______________________________

Trustee: ______________________________

Primary beneficiary/beneficiaries: ______________________________

Secondary beneficiary/beneficiaries: ______________________________

I am the primary beneficiary of the following property held in trust:

Property address: ______________________________

County: ______________________________

Grantor: ______________________________

Trustee: ______________________________

Secondary beneficiary/beneficiaries: ______________________________

Real Estate: Other Highlights

CHAPTER 9
MY OTHER ASSETS AND DEBTS

The preceding chapters provided checklists for you to record your checking, savings, and retirement accounts plus insurance, investments, and real estate: what most people first think about as their assets. This chapter provides places to list the common physical and digital assets that you might have—online accounts, vehicles, loyalty programs, and business interests you own—as well as debts you owe or are owed.

Take the time to think about all the personal assets you have, whether priceless heirlooms, irreplaceable family photographs, musical instruments, Beatles posters, or a special collection of model trains or shot glasses. You don't need to note every asset you own, as the listing could go on for pages.

Use these checklists to record information about any of these not-so-obvious assets. You may be surprised at what you have. The information will also be invaluable to your family, should something happen to you. Having an inventory of your belongings can save your executor time and your estate money. This information can help avoid surprises—and executors don't like surprises when it comes time to finalizing an estate. A big plus in assembling this information now is it can motivate you to take stock of what you have. This is practical information that you will refer to frequently and need to keep up to date.

Here you can also note your virtual assets. Your iTunes, photo storage, ebooks, loyalty airline and hotel rewards programs, as well as your Facebook, Twitter, and other social media sites have value, even if not in a strictly monetary sense.

You will also find checklists for your debts, including financial obligations such as credit cards and money you have borrowed from others. Sad but true: your creditors will need to be paid before your family members will be able to receive their inheritance.

My To-Do Checklist

Done	Need to Do	
❑	❑	List and assemble receipts or appraisals for valuable possessions
❑	❑	Photograph or videotape special possessions
❑	❑	Write down stories behind your special possessions
❑	❑	Identify who you want to get special items
❑	❑	Label photographs
❑	❑	Inventory your digital assets
❑	❑	Put the terms of any personal loans in writing
❑	❑	List contact information for credit cards
❑	❑	Note details of a reverse mortgage
❑	❑	Complete the checklists for Chapter 9

✔ List and assemble receipts or appraisals for valuable possessions

The checklists in this chapter provide space for you to list any assets of value you may own. You don't need to list everything, but do include items of special interest or great value, such as furniture, paintings and other artwork, coin and stamp collections, jewelry, and musical instruments. You'll also want to find receipts or appraisals, which are important in establishing the value of your special possessions. If you don't have those and want to establish value, you can get your items appraised. This will help if you need to file an insurance claim for loss or theft.

✔ Photograph or videotape special possessions

Along with your list and receipts and appraisals, you may want to take photographs or make a video as you walk through your rooms, closets, cabinets, attic, garage, and basement. Store the photos or video in the cloud or in your safe deposit box or other fireproof storage. This documentation will be valuable in filing an insurance claim or helping your executor prepare an estate inventory.

✔ Write down the stories behind the possessions

After you have listed and photographed or videotaped the items, go the extra step to capture any interesting stories about how you acquired special items. You can do this while you video the items, or by writing stories by hand or on a computer, or by dictating them to a family member. Only you will be able to pass on the history of the silver bowl you got as a wedding present from Aunt Tully or how you haggled with a street merchant for the painting in the dining room. Be sure your family knows that the opal ring came from your maternal grandmother, while the pocket watch was Great Uncle Randolph's. I hired my teenaged granddaughter to take the pictures and write down notes on where the items came from and why they were important. She was a big help in getting the job done and reaching things on high shelves, and she appreciated learning a lot of family history—and earning a little spending money.

✔ Identify who will get special items

Once you have taken your inventory of special items, think about whom you want to give them to. Make a list describing each item and whom you want to receive it. This list, sometimes called a ***letter of instruction***, tells your executor how you want personal items distributed upon your death. Sign and date the letter and put it with your will, although it's not formally part of your will. It can be extremely helpful in both reducing family disagreements as to who gets what and in letting your executor know your wishes. And there may be items you want to gift before you die. Are there things you want family members or friends to enjoy now? Instead of hanging on to something you don't need or use, give your granddaughter the special earrings so you can enjoy seeing her wear them now.

✔ Label the photographs

Years from now your grandkids won't remember whether the family photograph hanging on the bedroom wall is from your side of the family or your spouse's side. A note on the back of the frame that says when and where the picture was taken and who's in the picture will be greatly appreciated. If you don't recognize someone, ask others who might know. The next generation will have an even harder time tracking the information down.

Going through those boxes and albums of stored family photographs may take time, but you'll probably have fun and raise some fond memories. If you can't identify who's in the picture, you can be sure your kids won't have a clue. I've just gone through a cedar chest full of my in-laws' framed family photos. For too many of them, I wish I knew more about the family stories behind the pictures.

✔ Inventory your digital assets

In this digital age, your online assets can be as valuable as your physical property. User IDs and their associated passwords are essential to gain access to e-mail, electronic banking, online bill paying, bitcoins, iTunes, e-books, games, Facebook, LinkedIn, Twitter, PayPal, movies, videos, digital photo storage, and shopping sites, to name just some of the most obvious. You may have a username and password to access your benefit information at MyMedicare.gov and My SocialSecurity.gov, or a TreasuryDirect account. Many of our business and personal records and files are found or stored online. Even the checklists in this book, containing valuable information, can be downloaded at **ambar.org/AARPForms** so that you can access, update, and store them on your computer.

The first thing you want to do is create a list of your online accounts with usernames and passwords. Be sure to keep it in a secure place. Keeping that list up to date will save you time and frustration. And without it, your family will waste many hours trying to figure out basic information, such as if your utility bill is on automatic bill payment, or if your credit card bill has been paid, or even how to unlock your computer or smartphone.

Have you ever thought about what would happen to all that information if you become unable to use your computer and other electronic devices or when you die? Most websites and social media, as well as federal and state privacy and computer fraud laws, make it very difficult for anyone other than you to have access to your digital accounts and records. You want those security protections now, but in an emergency or after death, they can be huge barriers to your family or those you want to have access. Most current laws now criminalize, or at least penalize, unauthorized access of computers and digital accounts. Many digital providers are prohibited from disclosing most account information to anyone without the account holder's consent. And most sites aren't very clear, or are silent, about how you might go about giving consent to someone else to have access. Read the privacy or access policies of key websites to learn what they allow. Each site may have different procedures and steps you need to take.

States are beginning to pass laws about what happens to digital assets when the owner dies or is incapacitated. These laws give you the power to plan for the management and distribution of your digital assets just as you can plan for your tangible property by giving instructions in a will, trust, or power of attorney. You can, in your durable power of attorney or will (as I discuss in Chapter 10), authorize your agent or your executor to have access to your online accounts, for the limited purpose of carrying out fiduciary duties. For example, you can direct your executor to access your e-mail account to inventory your assets and to close the account in an orderly manner. You may want to prepare a special power of attorney just to give someone authority to manage your digital accounts. If there are certain accounts you don't want anyone else to access, put that in your document, too.

A word of caution: As valuable as this information is going to be to you and your family, it's a gold mine for identity thieves! Keep this checklist in a very secure place. You may want to tell just one or two trusted family members where it is located. Also remember that you need to keep it up to date. Changing our passwords frequently helps keep them secure.

✔ Put the terms of any personal loans in writing

Your family may have little knowledge of your debts. While you do not need to list fluctuating monthly bills, note in the checklist if you have borrowed money from or lent money to a relative, friend, or associate.

All personal loans should be in writing so that both the borrower and the lender have a record of the terms for paying back the money. If you intend to forgive any debts at your death, put your intentions in writing. Forgiving a loan becomes a gift, which can have consequences in settling your estate, determining taxes, and being eligible for Medicaid. (Refer to Chapter 3 for more information on Medicaid eligibility.)

✔ List contact information for credit cards

It's important that you have a list of all your credit card accounts and update these lists when you get new cards. Also list other authorized users for your credit cards. You need to have this list readily available now in case you need to report that a card has been lost or stolen. Later, your family members need this information so they will know what companies to contact after your death to close accounts. The credit card companies, as well as the credit reporting bureaus, will flag the accounts with a note that the owner is deceased. Sad as it may sound, identity thieves are known to read obituaries to seek potential victims. They'll try to use any still open credit card accounts of a dead person as long as they can get away with their thievery. They may also try to open new accounts knowing that a dead person doesn't check credit reports or open mail.

✔ Note if you have a reverse mortgage

A reverse mortgage is a special type of loan to help homeowners aged 62 or older borrow money against the equity in their home. Most reverse mortgages are Home Equity Conversion Mortgages or HECMs, which are federally insured and regulated loans by the U.S. Federal Housing Administration. A reverse mortgage is different from other types of loans because the borrower does not make payments during the loan as long as the homeowner lives there. This section gives you a brief overview, but be sure to do your own research to explore the pros and cons.

If you are eligible, you can get a reverse mortgage, like a traditional mortgage, from a private lender (such as a bank) that is secured by the equity in your house. Unlike a traditional mortgage that gets smaller as loan payments are made, the reverse mortgage typically gets larger over time because compound interest on the amount borrowed continues to increase the longer the loan is in place. You do not need to make payments until you die, move, or sell your home. After death, your estate pays back the mortgage plus interest accrued. This can be done by selling the house if there is any remaining equity or turning the house over to the lender if there is not.

Why is this? If your increasing loan balance grows so it equals or exceeds the value of your home, then your total debt is limited to your home's value, if your home is sold to repay the loan. If your family wishes to keep the home after you die or you move and pay off the loan with other proceeds, such as a new mortgage, you or your estate must pay the full loan balance.

Because reverse mortgages are quite different from any other loan, you need to do your homework carefully and thoroughly before considering one. As a protection to you so that you understand all the consequences and benefits of a reverse mortgage, you must receive independent counseling by a certified counselor before the lender can issue the loan. You can find a list of certified HECM counselors at https://entp.hud.gov/idapp/html/hecm_agency_look.cfm.

While the benefits of using your home's equity to meet expenses can be substantial, the upfront and ongoing costs involved in a reverse mortgage are high. These fees, including an origination fee, mortgage insurance premium, closing costs, and loan servicing fees, can amount to thousands of dollars. Unless you are facing a financial emergency, you may want to consider other options before taking out a reverse mortgage. Your family needs to know if you have a reverse mortgage on your home and realize that the loan must be repaid as soon as you die, move, or sell your home.

OTHER ASSETS AND DEBTS ACTION CHECKLISTS

The checklists in Chapter 9 are set out in the following order:

- *Business Interests*
- *Copyrights, Patents, and Royalties*
- *Credit/Debit Cards*
- *Digital Assets*
- *Lawsuits and Judgments*
- *Loyalty Programs*
- *Outstanding Loans*
- *Personal Debts*
- *Reverse Mortgage*
- *Special Possessions*
- *Storage Units*
- *Vehicles*
- *Assets and Debts: Other Highlights*

You can download these checklists in Word or fillable PDF format at **ambar.org/AARPforms**.

Business Interests

Business name: ______________________________

Type of business: ______________________________

Corporation: ______________________________

Partners: ______________________________

% of ownership: ______________________________

Phone: ______________________ Fax: ______________________

Address: ______________________________

Website: ______________________________

Business name: ______________________________

Type of business: ______________________________

Corporation: ______________________________

Partners: ______________________________

% of ownership: ______________________________

Phone: ______________________ Fax: ______________________

Address: ______________________________

Website: ______________________________

Where to find my business documents: ______________________

Copyrights, Patents, and Royalties

I have the following copyrights or patents:

Description:____________________________________

Date granted: ________________ Termination date: ________________

Status: ____________________________________

Copyright or patent #: ______________________________

Where to find information about my copyright or patent: ________________

Description:____________________________________

Date granted: ________________ Termination date: ________________

Status: ____________________________________

Copyright or patent #: ______________________________

Where to find information about my copyright or patent: ________________

I have the following royalty agreements:

Description:____________________________________

Date granted: ________________ Termination date: ________________

Status: ____________________________________

Royalty amount: ________________________________

Description:____________________________________

Date granted: ________________ Termination date: ________________

Status: ____________________________________

Royalty amount: ________________________________

Where to find information about my royalty: ________________________

Credit/Debit Cards

Name of credit/debit card: ____________________

Contact phone: ____________________

Website:____________________

Account number: ____________________

Card PIN: ____________________

Automatic payment:

- ❑ Paid from: ______________(bank account/credit card)
- ❑ Day of month deducted: ____________________

Other authorized users: ____________________

Name of credit/debit card: ____________________

Contact phone: ____________________

Website: ____________________

Account number: ____________________

Card PIN: ____________________

Automatic payment:

- ❑ Paid from: ______________(bank account/credit card)
- ❑ Day of month deducted: ____________________

Other authorized users: ____________________

Name of credit/debit card: ____________________

Contact phone: ____________________

Website: ____________________

Account number: ____________________

Card PIN: ______________________________

Automatic payment:

- ❑ Paid from: ______________(bank account/credit card)
- ❑ Day of month deducted: ______________________________

Other authorized users: ______________________________

Name of credit/debit card: ______________________________

Contact phone: ______________________________

Website:______________________________

Account number: ______________________________

Card PIN: ______________________________

Automatic payment:

- ❑ Paid from: ______________(bank account/credit card)
- ❑ Day of month deducted: ______________________________

Other authorized users: ______________________________

Name of credit/debit card: ______________________________

Contact phone: ______________________________

Website:______________________________

Account number: ______________________________

Card PIN: ______________________________

Automatic payment:

- ❑ Paid from: ______________(bank account/credit card)
- ❑ Day of month deducted: ______________________________

Other authorized users: ______________________________

Where to find my usernames and passwords for online access: ______________________

Digital Assets

Word of caution: Carefully secure this list!

Fiduciary or agent who has access to my digital assets: ______________________________

Website/app: ____

Username: ____________________________ Password: ______________________________

Security questions and answers: ____

Website: ____

Username: ____________________________ Password: ______________________________

Security questions and answers: ____

Website: ____

Username: ____________________________ Password: ______________________________

Security questions and answers: ____

Website: ____

Username: ____________________________ Password: ______________________________

Security questions and answers: ____

Website: ____

Username: ____________________________ Password: ______________________________

Security questions and answers: ____

Website: ____

Username: ____________________________ Password: ______________________________

Security questions and answers: ____

Website:____

Username: ______________________ Password: ______________________

Security questions and answers: ______________________________

Website:____

Username: ______________________ Password: ______________________

Security questions and answers: ______________________________

Website:____

Username: ______________________ Password: ______________________

Website:____

Username: ______________________ Password: ______________________

Security questions and answers: ______________________________

Website:____

Username: ______________________ Password: ______________________

Security questions and answers: ______________________________

Website:____

Username: ______________________ Password: ______________________

Security questions and answers: ______________________________

Website:____

Username: ______________________ Password: ______________________

Security questions and answers: ______________________________

Lawsuits and Judgments

I have the following lawsuits or legal claims pending:

Case name: ______________________________

Court: ______________________________

Attorney: ______________________________

Type lawsuit or legal claim: ______________________________

Case name: ______________________________

Court: ______________________________

Attorney: ______________________________

Type lawsuit or legal claim: ______________________________

I have the following uncollected legal judgments pending:

Case name: ______________________________

Court: ______________________________

Attorney: ______________________________

Type of judgment: ______________________________

Amount of judgment: ______________________________

Case name: ______________________________

Court: ______________________________

Attorney: ______________________________

Type of judgment: ______________________________

Amount of judgment: ______________________________

Loyalty Programs

Airline: ______________________________

Website: ______________________________

Rewards #: ______________________________

Username: ____________ Password/PIN: ____________

Airline: ______________________________

Website: ______________________________

Rewards #: ______________________________

Username: ____________ Password/PIN: ____________

Train: ______________________________

Website: ______________________________

Rewards #: ______________________________

Username: ____________ Password/PIN: ____________

Hotel: ______________________________

Website: ______________________________

Rewards #: ______________________________

Username: ____________ Password/PIN: ____________

Hotel: ____

Website: ____

Rewards #: ____

Username: ____________________ Password/PIN: ____________________

Store: ____

Website: ____

Rewards #: ____

Username: ____________________ Password/PIN: ____________________

Store: ____

Website: ____

Rewards #: ____

Username: ____________________ Password/PIN: ____________________

Store: ____

Website: ____

Rewards #: ____

Username: ____________________ Password/PIN: ____________________

Car rental: ____

Website: ____

Rewards #: ____

Username: ____________________ Password/PIN: ____________________

Car rental company: ______________________________

Website: ______________________________

Rewards #: ______________________________

Username: ______________ Password/PIN: ______________

Company: ______________________________

Website: ______________________________

Rewards #: ______________________________

Username: ______________ Password/PIN: ______________

Company: ______________________________

Website: ______________________________

Rewards #: ______________________________

Username: ______________ Password/PIN: ______________

Company: ______________________________

Website: ______________________________

Rewards #: ______________________________

Username: ______________ Password/PIN: ______________

Outstanding Loans

The following people owe me money:

Name of borrower: ______________________________

Contact phone: ______________________________

Address: ______________________________

Amount due: ______________________________

Where to find loan documents: ______________________________

Name of borrower: ______________________________

Contact phone: ______________________________

Address: ______________________________

Amount due: ______________________________

Where to find loan documents: ______________________________

Name of borrower: ______________________________

Contact phone: ______________________________

Address: ______________________________

Amount due: ______________________________

Where to find loan documents: ______________________________

Name of borrower: ______________________________

Contact phone: ______________________________

Address: ______________________________

Amount due: ______________________________

Where to find loan documents: ______________________________

Personal Debts

I owe the following people or entities money:

Internal Revenue Service: ______________________________

Contact phone: ______________________________

Address: ______________________________

Amount due: ______________________________

Where to find debt documents: ______________________________

State Department of Taxation: ______________________________

Contact phone: ______________________________

Address: ______________________________

Amount due: ______________________________

Where to find debt documents: ______________________________

Name of lender: ______________________________

Contact phone: ______________________________

Address: ______________________________

Amount due: ______________________________

Where to find debt documents: ______________________________

Name of lender: ______________________________

Contact phone: ______________________________

Address: ______________________________

Amount due: ______________________________

Where to find debt documents: ______________________________

Name of lender: ______________________________

Contact phone: ______________________________

Address: ______________________________

Amount due: ______________________________

Where to find debt documents: ______________________________

Reverse Mortgage

Property address: ______________________________

Financial institution: ______________________________

Phone: ____________________ Fax: ____________________

Address: ______________________________

E-mail: ____________________ Website: ____________________

Type of reverse mortgage: ______________________________

Mortgage account #: ______________________________

Special Possessions

I have the following special possessions, including antiques, jewelry, art, furniture, silver, and musical instruments:

Item description: ______________________________

Value: $__________ Where to find the receipt or appraisal: ______________

Item description: ______________________________

Value: $__________ Where to find the receipt or appraisal: ______________

Item description: ______________________________

Value: $__________ Where to find the receipt or appraisal: ______________

Item description: ______________________________

Value: $__________ Where to find the receipt or appraisal: ______________

Item description: ______________________________

Value: $__________ Where to find the receipt or appraisal: ______________

Item description: ______________________________

Value: $__________ Where to find the receipt or appraisal: ______________

Item description: ______________________________

Value: $__________ Where to find the receipt or appraisal: ______________

Item description: ______________________________

Value: $__________ Where to find the receipt or appraisal: ______________

Item description: ______________________________

Value: $__________ Where to find the receipt or appraisal: ______________

Item description: ______________________________

Value: $__________ Where to find the receipt or appraisal: ______________

Storage Units

Storage company: ____

Address: ____

Unit #: ____

Website: ____

Monthly rent: $ ____

Automatic payment:

- ❑ Paid from: ______________(bank account/credit card)
- ❑ Day of month deducted: ___________

Items in storage unit: ____

____

Storage company: ____

Address: ____

Unit #: ____

Website: ____

Monthly rent: $ ____

Automatic payment:

- ❑ Paid from: ______________(bank account/credit card)
- ❑ Day of month deducted: ___________

Items in storage unit: ____

____

Storage company: ____

Address: ____

Unit #: ____

Website: ____

Monthly rent: $ ____

Automatic payment:

- ❑ Paid from: _____________(bank account/credit card)
- ❑ Day of month deducted: __________

Items in storage unit: ____

____

Where to find the key or lock combination: ______________________________

Vehicles

(Include cars, trucks, recreational vehicles, boats, campers, and other vehicles)

Make: ____________________ Model: ____________________

Year: __________ Tag #: ____________________

Where to find title: ____________________

Make: ____________________ Model: ____________________

Year: __________ Tag #: ____________________

Where to find title: ____________________

Make: ____________________ Model: ____________________

Year: __________ Tag #: ____________________

Where to find title: ____________________

Make: ____________________ Model: ____________________

Year: __________ Tag #: ____________________

Where to find title: ____________________

Make: ____________________ Model: ____________________

Year: __________ Tag #: ____________________

Where to find title: ____________________

Make: ____________________ Model: ____________________

Year: __________ Tag #: ____________________

Where to find title: ____________________

Assets and Debts: Other Highlights

CHAPTER 10
MY WILL, TRUST, AND POWER OF ATTORNEY FOR FINANCES

Many people think an "estate" is just for those with million-dollar houses, fancy cars, and lots of money. Not so. "Estate" is simply a term for the money and property you have when you die.

No matter how large or small your estate, you'll need a few legal documents in place to set out your wishes for how you want your estate distributed after your death. That's what I cover in this chapter. Pulling together these documents ensures that things go where you want and your family doesn't have to make decisions during a traumatic time. These documents also can help save money on lawyers and probate.

A ***will***—or, more technically, your last will and testament—is the primary document you use to specify who you want to receive what. You use a ***codicil*** to amend your will when circumstances change your plan. Depending on your circumstances, you can create a living trust as a companion to your will to direct how you want your money and property managed and distributed both before and after your death.

While you may find online forms, to get these documents done right, I recommend talking with experts in estate planning and taxes. You want to make sure you have all the documents you need for your unique situation and that each document is drafted and executed properly. This chapter walks you through the process and provides you with an opportunity to review the documents you have (or need) and indicate where your family can find them.

My To-Do Checklist

Done	Need to Do	
❑	❑	Know the basics of estate planning
❑	❑	Understand what probate is and does
❑	❑	Identify a source of funding for costs to close your estate
❑	❑	Prepare or review your will
❑	❑	Prepare any necessary codicils to your will
❑	❑	Consider if a living trust should be part of your estate plan
❑	❑	Select an agent to manage your financial affairs
❑	❑	Prepare a letter of instruction
❑	❑	Discuss your plan with those who need to know
❑	❑	Complete the checklists for Chapter 10

✔ Know the basics of estate planning

There is more to estate planning than writing a will. The first step is to review what you own, including bank accounts, investments, personal property, and real estate, and what you owe (or will owe), such as mortgages, debts, medical bills, and funeral expenses. Because you have filled out all the checklists in the previous chapters, you've completed that big first step.

The next step is to group your assets, as explained below, so you can make sure what you have gets where you want it to go.

- Your ***estate*** is everything you own at the time of your death.
- Your ***probate estate*** includes those things that will be distributed according to the directions in your will or, if you don't have a will, the distribution laws of your state.
- Your ***non-probate estate*** is everything that you have previously determined is not in your probate estate. You take something out of your probate estate by owning property jointly with rights of survivorship; by transferring property into a trust; and by indicating a beneficiary of your life insurance, annuities, investment accounts, and retirement funds. You can also take property out of your probate estate by deeding it to a trust (more on that later in this chapter). In these cases, your deed, trust, or other documents determine how those assets are distributed.
- Your ***taxable estate*** includes those assets that the federal government or your state can tax.

As you do estate planning, you need to appreciate the differences. Not everything in your estate is part of your probate estate, and not everything in your estate is subject to taxes.

✔ Understand what probate is and does

Probate is the court procedure that determines the validity of your will (if any), determines who will be in charge of settling your affairs, identifies your heirs, inventories your probate assets, determines claims against your estate, calculates any taxes to be paid, and makes sure the remaining proceeds are distributed to the proper people or organizations. In your will, you establish who gets what and how much. If you don't have a will, the court will apply your state's intestacy law to determine who gets what, as explained in Chapter 8. In effect, the probate court makes sure that your wishes are carried out, supervises how your estate is distributed, adjudicates any disputes over the terms of your will or claims against your estate, and sorts out family disagreements.

Much has been written about the cost of probate, and you may have heard that it should be avoided at all costs. In reality, going through probate means simply settling your estate through court supervision. It does incur fees and costs that cannot be avoided, but you can control some of the expense through advance preparation. Some minor costs of the probate process include filing fees to open the probate case by presenting your will and publishing legal notices in newspapers. Some states may also charge other filing fees for the inventory or accountings your personal representative files.

✔ Identify a source of funding for costs to close your estate

The major expenses in settling your estate—with or without probate court involvement—are professional fees for an attorney, real estate agent, appraiser, accountant, or tax preparer. The attorney for your estate advises the executor of your will or administrator of your estate (your personal representative), assists in filing court documents, and represents your estate in any disputes. Any professional fees will be paid as an expense of your estate. The more complex your financial affairs are and the less clear your wishes, the higher the professional fees will be.

Another major expense in settling your estate could be compensation for your personal representative. You can say in your will that your executor is not to be paid, but before adding that provision, think about all the work that is needed.

Otherwise, depending on the laws of your state, your personal representative will be paid either a percentage of the inventory value of your estate or a set fee determined by the judge or what is considered "just and reasonable." States that use a percentage to calculate the fee typically use a sliding scale. As the size of the estate increases, a smaller percentage is taken from the greater portions of the estate. For example, a personal representative might be entitled to a fee of 5 percent on the first $10,000 of an estate, 4 percent of the next $25,000, 3 percent of the next $50,000, and 2 percent of anything over $85,000.

States that base the personal representative's fee on what would be "just and reasonable" look at the work that needs to be done. The amount of work involved by two personal representatives can differ considerably even for estates of the same value. It is much simpler—and less expensive—to administer an estate if assets can be readily found, no claims against the estate need to be resolved, and no family squabbles need to be negotiated.

No matter how your personal representative is paid, you can make the job much easier and often less expensive by completing the checklists in this book. The more advance work you do, the less time your personal representative must spend. And the clearer your wishes will be.

✔ Prepare or review your will

A will, or last will and testament, is the legal document by which you set out who you want to receive your probate estate. By intestacy law, your spouse or other blood relatives would inherit your estate. If you want someone who is not related to you to receive any of it, you need a will. By having a will, you can also make sure that someone (other than your spouse) who would inherit if you don't have a will does not.

In your will, you set out who your beneficiaries are and what you want them to receive. You can make gifts in your will of specific items, such as your car or wedding ring; or a set dollar amount; or percentages divided among several friends or relatives. Another way to establish who is to get some of your personal property is to write a letter of instruction that is separate from your will; I explain this later in this chapter.

Your will can also indicate donations to the charities, schools, or religious groups you support, letting you take advantage of tax laws that encourage private philanthropy.

You can name the person you want to be in charge of managing your estate, and the court will appoint that person as your executor. If you have not nominated an executor in your will, the court will appoint an administrator for you. The duties of your personal representative, whether called an executor or administrator, are the same.

You should choose your personal representative with care because that person has many responsibilities. It can be a big task that requires good financial skills, attention to detail, patience, and probably a dose of diplomacy. Your personal representative must inventory your assets, have them appraised, pay bills, publish legal notices, prepare your final income tax return, work with financial institutions to close out accounts, record documents to sell or transfer real estate, find and notify beneficiaries, file any estate tax returns, and file inventories and accountings with the court. All the while your personal representative must keep happy the anxious and impatient debtors and beneficiaries of your estate. It's a good idea to name a successor executor in case the person you name becomes unable to serve.

If you have minor children, you can name in your will who you would like to be their guardian. Be sure to talk this through with any people you are considering to make sure they are willing and able to take on this responsibility. If you wish to leave assets to any minors, you'll want to create a testamentary trust, which is set up and funded as part of your will and comes into effect after your death. With this legal document, minors' inheritances can be managed until they reach the age of majority by the trustee you select.

✔ Prepare any necessary codicils to your will

It is a good idea to review your will every few years, especially whenever the tax laws or your personal or family circumstances change. Consult with your lawyer to make sure your will continues to express your estate plan.

A ***codicil*** is the document that amends your will. As circumstances change, such as a death, divorce, or birth in your family, you may want to change a part of your will. You may want to add a bequest for a new grandchild or change your executor.

It can be easier to draft a codicil rather than rewriting and re-executing your entire will. But this is not a do-it-yourself project. Do not make any changes directly on your will. Strike-outs, erasures, and any other markings on your will can have the devious effect of invalidating your will. A codicil must be executed with the same formality, number of witnesses, and notary requirements as your will.

✔ Consider whether a living trust should be part of your estate plan

A living trust is a legal arrangement in which you transfer your interest in property so it can be managed for you. It is called a living trust because you create it while you are still alive. The trustee you select manages your trust assets while you are living as well as after your death. In addition to creating the trust document, you must also "fund" the trust by preparing deeds, retitling assets, reassigning brokerage accounts, or taking other steps to transfer ownership of the property you want in the trust. Because you must transfer legal ownership to the trust, the property in the trust no longer legally belongs to you and, therefore, is not part of your probate assets.

Every trust has three parties: the creator, the trustee, and the beneficiary or beneficiaries, although the same individual can be all three at the same time. You can name yourself as trustee because you want to manage the trust as long as you can. You name a successor trustee who takes over the trust management when you no longer are willing or able to and upon your death. You can also name yourself as the principal trust beneficiary so you can receive the trust proceeds to support yourself while you are living. You would name secondary beneficiaries with instructions on when and how the trust assets are to be managed and distributed after your death. In this way, your trust serves a remarkably similar purpose to your will in identifying how any trust assets are distributed to the beneficiaries you have named. Because any assets you have transferred to the trust are not part of your probate estate, your trust, rather than your will, controls how those assets are distributed.

A trust can be an important component to your estate plan. Whether you should have a trust, in addition to your will, depends on many personal factors. If you have substantial property that you may not be able to manage if you become incapacitated, you may want to set up a trust. If a trustee manages your assets, your family may not need to have a guardian appointed to oversee your estate if you become mentally or physically unable to do so yourself. By placing real estate that you own in another state into a trust, you may be able to avoid going through probate in the other state.

You should discuss with your estate planner whether a trust would be appropriate in your circumstances and what assets might best be placed into a trust. Be sure to find out if placing your home in a living trust would jeopardize any homestead exemption, impact eligibility for Medicaid, or increase your property taxes. Putting property into a living trust does not reduce your income or estate taxes. It also does not protect your property from creditors. You will still need a will for any property not held by your trust.

You may want to consider setting up a trust to provide for the care of your pets. According to ASPCA, all states have adopted pet trust laws. These laws specifically allow you to name your pet as a beneficiary of a trust so you can ensure that funds are available for its care. To read about your state's pet trust laws, visit www.aspca.org/pet-care/pet-planning/pet-trust-laws.

✔ Select an agent to manage your financial affairs

A ***power of attorney for finances*** is the legal document that lets you name an agent to manage your financial affairs. It is effective only during your lifetime. By creating a power of attorney while you have the ability to do so, you select the trustworthy individual—called your ***agent*** or ***attorney-in-fact***—you want to manage your financial affairs if you become unable to do so yourself. A power of attorney can give you peace of mind that if you should become unable to take care of your financial details for any reason, the person you choose will have the authority to start acting on your behalf.

You determine the specific responsibilities and duties you want your agent to have. You may want to give your agent general powers to do everything that you could do, or you may want to give specific powers. You should design your power of attorney to fit your anticipated needs. Among the powers that you can delegate to another are the responsibility to manage your investments, pay your bills, collect your debts, sue on your behalf, sell your real estate, negotiate with insurance companies, sell your car, or have access to bank accounts or digital assets. You may want your agent to sign your income tax returns, apply for benefits on your behalf, or make gifts to your favorite charities. If you want your agent to be able to make gifts of your money, you need to be very specific about how those gifts are to be made. As with other representatives you choose when planning your estate, you'll want to talk with your agent early and often about your expectations. Go over each part of the document to elaborate on what you do or do not want your agent to do when making decisions for you. Your agent needs to have a copy of the document even if he or she is not yet making any decisions.

Powers of attorney can differ depending on when you want your agent to be able to act for you.

- A ***durable*** power of attorney begins when you sign it and stays in effect for your lifetime—even after you become incapacitated—unless you cancel it. In some states, you must put specific words in the document stating that you want your agent's powers to stay in effect even if you become incapacitated. If you want this feature, it's very important that you have these words in your document. In the 29 states that have adopted the Uniform Power of Attorney Act, you do not need to be concerned about including the "durable" language; the law presumes that you want your agent to act after you become incapacitated. Check with a lawyer in your state.
- A ***springing*** power of attorney "springs" into effect at some time after you have signed the document, at a trigger you specify. You state in your power of attorney when you want your agent to begin to act. Your lawyer must carefully draft a springing power of attorney to avoid any difficulty in determining exactly when the springing event has happened.

Even if you sign a power of attorney, you can still manage your own affairs. You are not giving up anything. Think of a power of attorney as an extra set of car keys that you give to someone else. You have your own keys and determine when that extra set of keys can be used. When you can't or don't want to drive yourself, someone else has the keys to do the driving for you.

You can cancel, or revoke, a power of attorney at any time by tearing it up, signing a new one, or writing on it that you want to cancel it. You don't have to give any reason. If you change your mind about who you want to be your agent, you can create a new document. If you do cancel your power of attorney or change agents, be sure to let your agent and anyone your agent has been dealing with know that you have cancelled that agent's authority. Just like your will, it is important to review your power of attorney every few years or when your circumstances change. If you move to a new state, it's a good idea to have a lawyer in that state review your powers of attorney.

All powers of attorney come to an end upon your death. Your agent will have no authority to make any decisions after you die. Likewise, the executor you name in your will has no authority to act before your death.

Carefully consider whom you want to be your agent. Select someone you trust completely and who can do the job. It is best to avoid someone who is ill, inexperienced in financial matters, has a hard time managing his or her own money, or who for some other reason would not be able to carry out the responsibilities. Remember you are giving your agent the opportunity to act for you at a time when you may not be able to keep tabs on what the agent is doing. To that end, you may want to add ways for other people to check up on your agent when you cannot. It is prudent to name someone as an alternative agent in case the person you first name becomes unable to serve.

If you want your agent to have access to your bank account, be sure to get your bank's authorization forms and a signature card for your agent. Typically, a bank has its own form it wants your agent to sign before giving your agent access to a particular account. If you and your agent do not contact the bank before you become incapacitated, the bank may not honor checks or withdrawals your agent signs.

Giving your agent the authority to access your bank account is not the same as making someone a joint owner of the account. You'll want to make sure that you create the right kind of account so your agent has access to your funds to pay your bills but is not listed as an owner. Your bank may call this an agency, fiduciary, or convenience account. See Chapter 4 for a refresher on the various types of bank accounts and why they make a difference.

Powers of attorney for health care are addressed in Chapter 11.

✔ Prepare a letter of instruction

A letter of instruction serves as guidance to your family and your personal representative about matters they must attend to after your death and how you want specific personal possessions divided. This informal document can be attached to your will, though it is not an official part of it. You don't need a lawyer to prepare it, and you don't need to follow any legal format. Although it doesn't carry the legal weight of a will and is in no way a substitute for one, a letter of instruction clarifies any special requests you want carried out when you die. Think of it as a flexible, informal supplement to your will that covers more personal information than what is typically included in a will. You can easily change it as your circumstances or wishes change. All you need to do is sign and date your new letter.

Your letter of instruction can have two parts that do two different things:

1. One part offers instructions on your funeral. You might include instructions about the type of funeral or memorial service you want, who should officiate, who you want as pallbearers, or what songs should—or should not—be sung. You need to let your family know about your plans with the funeral home and whether you have already paid for any of the arrangements. Describe the location of any pre-purchased burial plot or crypt and where you keep the plot deed. If you want to be cremated, your family needs to know where you want your ashes scattered. (You can detail much of this information in Chapter 11.)
2. The other part of your letter of instruction specifies any special gifts of personal items you'd like to make. (You can also do this in your will.) We all have heard stories of family fights erupting over how to divide family pictures, jewelry, the stamp collection, or the wedding gift from Aunt Sue. The items may not have monetary value but getting them to the right people can make a big difference to you and to them. Your letter of instruction can help eliminate family feuds over who receives your personal items.

If you want to make sure that your granddaughter gets the pearl necklace you got for your high school graduation, or you have already promised your best friend your figurine collection, put your wishes in your letter. If you have any preferences as to who should get what, write it down. Be sure to leave instructions about care for your pets.

You can make your letter personal, too. You can use it to send important messages to your survivors. You might include special hopes you have for your grandchild's education or the important values you want to pass on. This could be the place to tell your family something you never got around to saying. It can be whatever you want it to be. You may also want to consider preparing an ethical will discussed in Chapter 11.

Your wishes can change over time. Revisit your instructions every couple of years or when your circumstances change. Always sign and date each revision to eliminate confusion over which is your most current statement. Just make sure your latest instructions are clear. Discard any older versions so there's no confusion about which version is the right one.

✔ Discuss your plans with those who need to know

Be sure you have talked with those you want to serve as the executor of your will, your children's guardian, your minors' trustee, your successor trustee for your living trust, and your power of attorney for finances to make sure they are willing and able to take on these responsibilities and fully understand what is required of them.

And be sure your loved ones know where all your documents are located. Some documents will be with your lawyer, others will be in your safe deposit box, and some will need to be on hand where your family can find them when decisions need to be made on your behalf. That's what the What to Find it checklist in Chapter 1 is for.

WILL, TRUST, AND POWER OF ATTORNEY FOR FINANCES ACTION CHECKLISTS

The checklists in Chapter 10 are set out in the following order:

- *Letters of Instruction*
- *Living Trust*
- *Power of Attorney for Finances*
- *Will and Codicil*
- *Will, Trust, and Power of Attorney for Finances: Other Highlights*

You can download these checklists in Word or fillable PDF format at **ambar.org/AARPforms**.

Letters of Instruction

I have a letter of instruction concerning the distribution of my personal possessions.

Where to find my letter of instruction: ______________________________

Date of my letter of instruction: ______________________________

I have a letter of instruction concerning my end-of-life preferences.

Where to find my letter of instruction: ______________________________

Date of my letter of instruction: ______________________________

Living Trust

Trustee: ______________________________

Phone: ______________________ E-mail: ______________________

Address: ______________________________

Successor trustee: ______________________________

Phone: ______________________ E-mail: ______________________

Address: ______________________________

Drafting lawyer: ______________________________

Phone: ______________________ E-mail: ______________________

Address: ______________________________

Where to find my living trust: ______________________________

Power of Attorney for Finances

- ❑ I have discussed my expectations with my agent.
- ❑ My power of attorney is "durable," meaning I intend that my agent act when I am incapacitated.
- ❑ My power of attorney is "springing," meaning my agent's authority begins: ___________
- ❑ My agent has a copy of my power of attorney.

Agent: ____

Phone: ______________________ E-mail: ______________________

Address: ____

Alternate agent: ____

Phone: ______________________ E-mail: ______________________

Address: ____

Date signed: ____

Drafting lawyer: ____

Will and Codicil

Executor: ______________________________

Phone: ______________ E-mail: ______________

Address: ______________________________

Alternative executor: ______________________________

Phone: ______________ E-mail: ______________

Address: ______________________________

Drafting lawyer: ______________________________

Phone: ______________ E-mail: ______________

Address: ______________________________

The original of my will is located: ______________________________

Copies of my will are located: ______________________________

I have executed the following codicil:

Codicil date: ______________________________

Drafting lawyer: ______________________________

Phone: ______________ E-mail: ______________

Address: ______________________________

Executor (if changed): ______________________________

Phone: ______________ E-mail: ______________

Address: ______________________________

Will, Trust, and Power of Attorney for Finances: Other Highlights

CHAPTER 11

MY MEDICAL AND FINAL WISHES

One of the kindest things that you can do for your family members is to spare them the distress of facing decisions about your health care and your final arrangements without knowing your wishes. You can do this by making those decisions yourself and sharing them. This chapter allows you to take both of those steps simply and easily.

Any time you become seriously ill—whatever your age—many decisions must be made about the medical care that you receive. As long as you are able to communicate your wishes, health care providers look to you for answers about what treatment choices you want. In those situations when you cannot communicate your wishes, decisions still need to be made. Your family and health care providers want to respect your treatment preferences, but they need to know ahead of time how to make the decisions you want them to make. Advance care planning involves thinking about what treatments and health care you do or do not want, communicating your thoughts to those who will be called upon to make decisions on your behalf, and, finally, putting those wishes down on paper in the appropriate legal forms.

In addition to knowing your wishes for your health care, your family members will need to make many decisions at the time of your death. You will be giving them a precious gift if you relieve them of any uncertainty about your wishes. By indicating on the checklists in this chapter what you want and the plans you have in place, your loved ones will be able to act with confidence that they are doing the right thing.

You may want a simple ceremony that celebrates your life or a more elaborate memorial service. If you are a veteran, you may want a military bugler with burial in a national cemetery. Many people have firm opinions about whether a casket should be open or closed.

Also, if you have prepaid for any part of your funeral or burial, your family members need to know about the pre-need contract so that they don't pay unnecessarily for anything you have already paid for. Decisions concerning the care of your body, including whether you want to be cremated or embalmed, are time sensitive. Your family also must know promptly upon your death if you wish to be an organ donor or if you have already arranged with a medical school to donate your body for medical research.

My To-Do Checklist

Done	Need to Do	
❑	❑	Select the person you want to be your health care agent
❑	❑	Consider preparing an ethical will
❑	❑	Prepare an organ donor card
❑	❑	Plan the disposition of your body
❑	❑	Plan your funeral
❑	❑	Consider options for paying for your funeral
❑	❑	Plan your final resting place
❑	❑	Complete the checklists for Chapter 11

✔ Select the treatments you do and don't want and the person you want to be your health care agent

An advance directive is a legally accepted and medically recognized way for you to let your family and health care providers know both the types of care you would want and who you want to make decisions about that care in the event you are unable to communicate.

Most people have heard of a ***living will***, yet it's only part of the instructions you can put into an advance directive. A living will outlines the treatments you would or would not want if you are unable to communicate and your death is imminent, or if you're permanently unconscious, in a vegetative state, or in the end-stage of a chronic condition such as Alzheimer's disease. You may want to talk with your doctor about these life-limiting conditions as defined by your state's laws.

In most states, the law restricts the circumstances under which a living will is effective. Typically, you can use it to document your wishes concerning specific end-of-life treatments. While it is crucial that your family and doctors understand your preferences concerning life-prolonging treatments, such as use of respirators, cardiopulmonary resuscitation, or intravenous nutrition or hydration, you may want to consider additional advance directives.

Because of these limitations of a living will, your advance directive can include a ***power of attorney for health care*** or ***health care proxy.*** In this more flexible advance directive, you select someone who can speak for you if you are unable to do so. In addition to specifying your end-of-life treatment preferences, you can give your agent broad authority to make any health care decision you specify, not about just life-prolonging treatments. You can set down any guidance or instructions you want your agent and your health care team to follow. And, perhaps more importantly, you can have someone who will speak for you and get necessary information from your health care providers to make the decisions you would want to be made. By having your preferences in writing and someone to speak up on your behalf, you can help your family make difficult decisions and make sure your personal values are respected.

Your agent should be someone who knows you and understands your wishes about medical treatments. You can authorize your agent to make decisions in situations you might not have anticipated. Your agent can talk with your health care providers about your changing medical condition and authorize treatment or have it withdrawn as circumstances change. In the sometimes-bewildering medical system, it is good to have someone in charge who can advocate for you. If health care providers resist following your wishes, your agent can stand up for what you want and take any other necessary steps to see that your wishes are honored. This includes changing doctors or hospitals, if necessary, to get the care you want.

When selecting your health care agent, you should choose someone you trust and who will be there for you now and well into the future. You will need to feel comfortable talking with your agent about your end-of-life care and confident that he or she will follow your wishes even if they are not similar to his or her own. Your agent should be able to be assertive, if necessary, when talking with health care professionals. Your choice also needs to meet your state's criteria for health care agents. Most states exclude some categories of people who can serve as agents—such as your doctor, the administrator of the nursing home where you are living, or someone else who works in your nursing home.

The first step in preparing an advance directive is to consider what you may want for medical care in the future. For many, this is not a simple step. It can be hard to foresee what your medical needs or problems might be at some unknown point in the future. You may want to talk with your family, doctor, spiritual advisers, or others who might be helpful in talking through serious medical issues and what brings quality to your life. The Five Wishes advance directive form at https://fivewishes.org/five-wishes/individuals-families/individuals-and-families may be helpful in starting and structuring important conversations about the medical care you wish to have. The American Bar Association also has a packet of resources that is very helpful in discussing with doctors and family your spiritual values, personal priorities, and more at www.americanbar.org/groups/law_aging/resources/health_care_decision_making/the-health-care-advance-planning-packet.

The next step is preparing your advance directive. You don't need a lawyer to draft this document. You can find state-specific forms at www.aarp.org/advancedirectives and links to other information about advance directives at ambar.org/HealthCarePOA. Many elder law attorneys will help you prepare your advance directives as part of your estate and advance care planning. Most hospitals, area agencies on aging, and medical societies also provide free forms.

Perhaps even more important than signing the document is the conversations you need to have with your health care agent. Your agent needs to understand what is important to you for your quality of life and the kind of medical care you would or would not want to have. Think of your advance directive as a written record of the conversations you have had with your agent about how you want to live up until the moment you die. Having your preferences in writing can be backup support for your agent and provide assurance that your wishes are known. It's a good idea to name someone as an alternative agent in case something should happen, and your first choice can't serve.

Your agent and your health care providers need to have copies of your advance directive. You may also wish to carry a wallet card that indicates you have an advance directive, where it's kept, and how to get in touch with your agent.

✔ Consider preparing an ethical will

Ethical wills may be a cherished and meaningful gift you can leave to your family. They are a way to share with your family, friends, and future generations your values, blessings, life's lessons, hopes and dreams for the future, love, and forgiveness. Preparing an ethical will is an opportunity to put down on paper what you hold dear—your memories, insights, values, and special wisdom that you don't want to be lost or forgotten.

Ethical wills are not new. They are an ancient tradition for passing on personal values, beliefs, blessings, and advice to future generations. Initially, ethical wills were transmitted orally. Over time, they evolved into written documents. You may want to create a video or audio recording of your ethical will as a cherished legacy for later generations. Ethical wills are not considered legal documents, unlike your living will and your last will and testament.

To help you get started, you can find examples of ethical wills and tips on how to prepare one at www.thelegacycenter.net/samples.html or www.life-legacies.com/ethicalwills.

✔ Prepare an organ donor card

Do you wish to share the gift of your organs or tissues with someone needing a transplant? These donations have saved or improved thousands of lives at absolutely no cost to the donor. Yet there is always a very long list of patients waiting for organ transplants. According to the U.S. Department of Health and Human Services, 109,000 men, women, and children were on the national waitlist as of September 2020.

If you do wish to give this gift, you need to sign and carry an organ donation card. In some states, you can indicate your wish to be an organ donor on your driver license. Most, but not all, states have an organ donation registry. You can find out if your state does at https://www.organdonor.gov/register.html. Sign up on your state's registry so your wishes can be honored. Make sure your family knows your wishes.

Most organ donations are made after a person has been declared brain dead following an accident, heart attack, or stroke. The organs or tissues are removed through a surgical procedure. Most organs must be transplanted within hours of the donation, while tissue donations of corneas, heart valves, skin, and bones can be preserved and stored in tissue banks. After the removal procedures, your body can be buried or cremated as though it were intact.

If you wish to make a ***whole body donation*** to a medical school or research facility, you need to make arrangements with the school or research entity before you die. Again, be sure to talk with your family members about your donation plan so they will know the specific instructions for how to transfer your body to the research facility. Typically, the facility will cremate your body at no expense and deliver your ashes as you instruct.

You and your family should be aware of the restrictions on transporting cremains. The U.S. Postal Service has strict rules requiring that cremains mailed through the post office be in a box with specific labels (Label 139) on all sides indicating that it contains cremated remains.

If you're traveling with cremains by air, check with the airlines ahead of time about restrictions such as whether to put the remains in carry-on luggage, a checked bag, or as cargo. The Transportation Safety Administration (TSA) requires the cremains to be an opaque container to go through security. My sister learned this the hard way when she was delayed at airport security while trying to fly with our mother's cremains in a granite urn.

✔ Plan the disposition of your body

You will need to decide what you wish to have done with your body after your death. Your choices may include being embalmed to delay decomposition of your body, a natural burial without embalming, burial in a coffin in a cemetery or in a crypt in a mausoleum, or cremation. If you prefer cremation, your ashes may be buried in an urn at a cemetery, placed in a columbarium, or scattered at the location of your choice.

If you wish your body to be buried, you will need to purchase a plot at a cemetery or a niche in a mausoleum. You can purchase just a single lot or multiple lots in a block where other family members would also be buried. When purchasing a cemetery lot, ask about any additional charges for the opening and closing and perpetual care of the site. You should receive a deed to the land, or plot, that you have purchased. The cost of cemetery lots varies significantly depending on where you wish to be buried. Be sure to record that information on the Burial checklist so your family knows that you have purchased a cemetery plot or crypt in a mausoleum.

More people are considering natural or "green" burials. With natural burial, your body would be promptly buried, without embalming, in the ground in a biodegradable coffin made of cardboard or bamboo or in a shroud.

You may want to have your body cremated after a funeral, or you may choose direct cremation, where your body goes directly from the place of death to the crematory. Before cremation, an official will need to prepare a death certificate and obtain a cremation permit. You may want to sign a pre-need authorization for cremation, appointing the person you want to consent to your cremation and to receive your ashes, or your spouse or next of kin will need to sign a consent about the disposition of your body. A funeral home or crematory should be able to give you a form for you to sign so you can make sure your wishes to be cremated are carried out. The Cremation Association of North America offers a list of its members and questions to ask cremation providers at cremationassociation.org.

Every state has regulations concerning the scattering of ashes, so check with your state agency that regulates burials. The scattering of ashes at sea must be done at least three nautical miles from land and the Environmental Protection Agency needs notice within thirty days following the event.

Those of certain faiths may have special rituals for washing the body, staying with the body until burial, and promptly burying the body without embalming.

Because of the many options, be sure your family knows of your wishes.

✔ Plan your funeral

How do you wish your death to be commemorated? Depending on your family and cultural or religious traditions, you may wish no service or ceremony, a lively gathering of family and friends to celebrate your life, a memorial service, a viewing at a mortuary, a wake, or a religious service in your place of worship. A funeral generally means that the body of the deceased is present, while a memorial service is held after the body has been buried or cremated.

A funeral director can help you plan for whatever type of commemoration you wish. You can discuss and even purchase the type of casket you would prefer, as well as other arrangements for any service or ceremony. Funeral directors must give you written price lists that tell you the costs for body preparation and transportation, caskets or urns, grave liners, and other services.

With the price lists in hand, you can comparison shop among several funeral homes to make sure you get the arrangements exactly as you desire and have a better idea about the range of costs. Keep in mind that you can choose where you purchase your casket or urn—even online; you needn't purchase it from the funeral home.

A funeral director can also help you arrange for a headstone or grave marker. While both identify the person buried, headstones typically extend above the ground and grave markers lie flat. Some cemeteries or memorial parks require grave markers to make it easier to care for the grounds. You can indicate on the Burial checklist the inscription you want on your headstone or grave marker.

✔ Consider options for paying for your funeral

Funerals are expensive—on average, $7,000. But there are ways to save your family from that financial burden.

Many funeral establishments let you pay a fixed price now for your funeral. Prepaying fixes the costs at today's prices for your choice of a casket and other services that may cost more in the future. Equally important, making your own financial arrangements gives you the peace of mind that your family will not have this burden.

Before prepaying for your funeral with a funeral director, get confirmation in writing about how your financial investment will be protected. You want to be assured that your money is in safe hands and your pre-need contract will be honored decades into the future. You pay most pre-need contracts in either a lump sum or installment payments. Your money is then placed in trust held by a third-party trustee or used to purchase an insurance policy. The trustee or insurance company is responsible for managing the money until it is time to pay the funeral home for the goods and services listed in your contract. Ask how your funds will be securely protected.

Also ask about the portability of your contract should the funeral home change hands or you move to another location and want your funeral there. In those cases, you'll want to be able to transfer the contract to a different funeral home.

Before paying for a pre-need contract, check with your state's attorney general or board of funeral directors to learn how pre-need contracts are regulated in your state. Your family will need to know if you have a pre-need contract, so include the details on the Funeral checklist.

Another option for making sure your family is not saddled with the expenses for your funeral is to purchase a life insurance policy that would cover the anticipated funeral costs, or invest in a certificate of deposit or savings account designated to cover these expenses, or put your money in a Pay on Death bank account (see Chapter 4). With options like these, you will know that the money will be available to your family, but you remain in control of the money until you die.

A note about bereavement fares: Most airlines used to offer bereavement fares so that immediate family members could save on the ticket price when they needed to fly on short notice because of a death in the family. Unfortunately, many airlines no longer offer bereavement fares. An airline booking agent may be able to help your family lower the cost of their flight. Online sites with last minute deals, such as Expedia, Hotwire, Kayak, Orbitz, Priceline, or Travelocity, may have lower last-minute prices.

MEDICAL AND FINAL WISHES ACTION CHECKLISTS

The checklists in Chapter 11 are set out in the following order:

- *Burial*
- *Celebration of Life*
- *Charities*
- *Cremation*
- *Donation of Organs and Tissues*
- *Entombment*
- *Ethical Will/Legacy Documents*
- *Final Wishes*
- *Funeral*
- *Health Care Directives*
- *Letters to Friends and Relatives*
- *Memorial Service*
- *Obituary*
- *People to Contact*
- *Pet Care*
- *Whole Body Donation*
- *Medical and Final Wishes: Other Highlights*

You can download these checklists in Word or fillable PDF format at **ambar.org/AARPforms**.

Burial

I own the following cemetery lot:

Ownership of the cemetery lot in the name of: ______________________

Location of lot:

Cemetery: ______________________

Section: ______________________ Lot: ______________________

Address: ______________________

____

Where to find the deed to my cemetery lot: ______________________

Other description:

____

____

____

____

____

❑ I would like a headstone.

❑ I would like a grave marker.

I would like these words on my grave marker or headstone:

____

____

____

____

I would like these symbols on my grave marker or headstone: ______________

I would like this type of casket:

____

____

____

Other burial instructions:

____

____

____

____

____

____

Celebration of Life

My wishes for a celebration of life ceremony:

Type of celebration: ______________________________

People to invite:

____

____

____

____

____

____

Location: ______________________________

Time of day: ______________________________

Food and beverages:

____

____

____

____

Entertainment or music:

____

____

____

____

- ❑ I have selected photos for the celebration.

Where to find them: ______________________________

Other requests for the celebration:

____

____

____

____

Notes for music I prefer:

____

____

____

____

Notes for any photos or videos:

____

____

____

____

Charities

I would appreciate memorial donations or gifts to the following charities:

Charity name: ______________________________

Contact information: ______________________________

Website:______________________________

Significance to me: ______________________________

Charity name: ______________________________

Contact information: ______________________________

Website:______________________________

Significance to me: ______________________________

Charity name: ______________________________

Contact information: ______________________________

Website:______________________________

Significance to me: ______________________________

Charity name: ______________________________

Contact information: ______________________________

Website:______________________________

Significance to me: ______________________________

Cremation

❑ I want my body to be cremated.

❑ I have signed a cremation authorization.

❑ I want my body to be cremated followed by a memorial service.

❑ I want my body to be cremated followed by a celebration of life service.

❑ I want my body to be cremated immediately upon my death.

Following my cremation, I wish my ashes to be disbursed as follows:

❑ To be scattered:

Location: ______________________________

❑ To be placed in an urn and buried or entombed:

Location: ______________________________

❑ Other:

____

❑ To be handled as my family sees fit.

I have made these prearrangements for my cremation:

Company: ______________________________

Address: ______________________________

Phone: ______________ Website: ______________

Where to find cremation prearrangements: ______________

Where to find cremation authorization: ______________

Donation of Organs and Tissues

❑ I wish to donate any needed organs or tissues.

❑ I wish to donate only the following organs or tissues:

Organs:

- ❑ Heart
- ❑ Kidneys
- ❑ Liver
- ❑ Lungs
- ❑ Pancreas
- ❑ Other ______________________________

Tissues:

- ❑ Blood vessels
- ❑ Bone
- ❑ Cartilage
- ❑ Corneas
- ❑ Heart valves
- ❑ Inner ear
- ❑ Intestines
- ❑ Skin
- ❑ Other ______________________________

I have a uniform donor card.

Where to find it: ______________________________

I have registered with my state's organ donation registry at this website:

____

Website username and password (if any): ______________________________

Entombment

I own the following crypt:

Ownership of the crypt in the name of: ______________________________

Location of crypt (church/mausoleum/columbarium): ______________________________

Address: ______________________________

Space #: ______________________________

Other description: ______________________________

Where to find deed: ______________________________

I would like the following words inscribed on the crypt:

____

____

Other instructions:

____

____

____

Ethical Will/Legacy Documents

I have created the following legacy documents:

Ethical will:

____

____

____

Where to find it: ______________________________

Legacy video:

____

____

____

Where to find it: ______________________________

Other legacy documents:

____

____

____

Who to receive my legacy documents: ____________________

____

____

Final Wishes

I wish to:

- ❑ Be embalmed (see the Cremation checklist)
- ❑ Be an organ donor (see the Donation of Organs and Tissues checklist)
- ❑ Have my body bequeathed to a medical school (see the Whole Body Donation checklist)
- ❑ Have my body buried in the earth (see the Burial checklist)
- ❑ Have my body entombed in a mausoleum (see the Entombment checklist)
- ❑ Be cremated (see the Cremation checklist)
- ❑ Other: ______________________________

I wish to have:

- ❑ A funeral service (see the Funeral checklist)
- ❑ A memorial service (see the Memorial Service checklist)
- ❑ A celebration of life service (see Celebration of Life checklist)
- ❑ A graveside service
- ❑ No service
- ❑ Other: ______________________________

My preferences are as follows:

____

____

____

____

____

Funeral

I have a pre-need contract and have prepaid for some or all of my funeral expenses.

Funeral director: ______________________________

Address: ______________________________

Phone: ______________ Website: ______________

Services selected and paid for:

____

____

____

____

Where to find pre-need contract: ______________________________

My wishes for the location of my funeral:

Funeral establishment: ______________________________

Address: ______________________________

Phone: ______________ E-mail: ______________

House of worship: ______________________________

Address: ______________________________

Phone: ______________ E-mail: ______________

Graveside: ______________________________

I wish the casket to be:

- ❑ Closed
- ❑ Open
- ❑ I prefer to wear: ______________________________

Religious leader/Officiant/Clergy:

____

____

____

____

Speakers/Readers:

____

____

____

____

Ushers/Pallbearers:

____

____

____

____

Favorite scripture, psalms, poems, readings:

____

____

____

____

Special hymns, music, musicians, soloists:

____

____

____

____

Health Care Directives

- ❑ I have a living will.
- ❑ I have a power of attorney for health care.
- ❑ I have talked with my health care agent about my medical preferences.

Health care agent: ____

Phone: ______________________ E-mail: ____________________________

Address: ____

I have given copies of my health care directives to the following:

- ❑ Health care agent: ____
- ❑ Physician: ____
- ❑ Physician: ____
- ❑ Physician: ____
- ❑ Hospital: ____
- ❑ Home health care agency: _______________________________________
- ❑ Residential care facility: _______________________________________
- ❑ Other: ____

Letters to Friends and Relatives

I have prepared letters for friends and relatives:

Person:____

Address: ____

Where to find letter: __________________________________

Person:____

Address: ____

Where to find letter: __________________________________

Person:____

Address: ____

Where to find letter: __________________________________

Person:____

Address: ____

Where to find letter: __________________________________

Person:____

Address: ____

Where to find letter: __________________________________

Memorial Service

My wishes for the location of my memorial service:

Funeral establishment: ______________________________

Address: ______________________________

Phone: ______________________ E-mail: ______________________

House of worship: ______________________________

Address: ______________________________

Phone: ______________________ E-mail: ______________________

Graveside: ______________________________

Religious leader/Officiant/Clergy:

____

____

Speakers/Readers:

____

____

____

____

Ushers/Pallbearers:

Favorite scripture, psalms, poems, readings:

Special hymns, music, musicians, soloists:

Obituary

I have written my own obituary.

Where to find it: ______________________________

I would like my obituary to appear in these newspapers and on these websites:

Newspaper: ______________________________

Newspaper: ______________________________

Website: ______________________________

Website: ______________________________

I would like the following information to appear in my obituary:

____

____

____

____

____

____

____

____

____

____

People to Contact

Please promptly inform the following people of my death:

Name: ______________________________

Relationship: ______________________________

Phone: ______________ E-mail: ______________

Address: ______________________________

Name: ______________________________

Relationship: ______________________________

Phone: ______________ E-mail: ______________

Address: ______________________________

Name: ______________________________

Relationship: ______________________________

Phone: ______________ E-mail: ______________

Address: ______________________________

Name: ______________________________

Relationship: ______________________________

Phone: ______________ E-mail: ______________

Address: ______________________________

Pet Care

I have made the following arrangements for the care of my pets.

____

____

____

I have made the following financial arrangements for the care of my pets.

____

____

____

I have a pet trust.

Where to find it: ______________________________________

____

Trustee: ____

Address: ____

Phone: ____________________ E-mail: ________________________

Whole Body Donation

I have made prearrangements with the following medical school or research organization:

Medical school or research organization: ______________________________

Address: ____

Phone: ____

Contact person: ______________________________________

Where to find confirmation of donation request: ______________________

Medical and Final Wishes: Other Highlights

RESOURCES

Books

Checklist for Family Survivors: A Guide to Practical and Legal Matters When Someone You Love Dies. Sally Balch Hurme. Published by AARP/the American Bar Association.

For My Grandchild. Published by AARP/Sterling.

Medicare for Dummies. Patricia Barry. Published by AARP/Wiley.

Navigating Your Later Years for Dummies. Carol Levine. Published by AARP/Wiley.

The Other Talk: A Guide to Talking with Your Adult Children about the Rest of Your Life. Tim Prosch. Published by AARP/McGraw-Hill.

Social Security for Dummies. Jonathan Peterson. Published by AARP/Wiley.

Websites

AARP, www.aarp.org

Aging Life Care Association, www.aginglifecare.org

Aging with Dignity, www.agingwithdignity.org

American Bar Association, www.americanbar.org

American Institute of CPAs, www.aicpa.org

Caring Connections, www.caringinfo.org

Centers for Medicare and Medicaid Services, www.medicare.gov

Certified Financial Planners, www.cfp.net

Financial Planning Association, www.plannersearch.org

Five Wishes, www.agingwithdignity.org/five-wishes.php

Funeral Consumer Alliance, www.funerals.org

National Academy of Elder Law Attorneys, www.naela.org

National Association of Estate Planners & Councils, www.naepc.org

National Guardianship Association, www.guardianship.org

Social Security Administration, www.ssa.gov

U.S. Department of Veterans Affairs, www.va.gov

ABOUT THE AUTHOR

Sally Balch Hurme, J.D., is author of the bestselling American Bar Association/AARP Checklist series. In addition to this updated *Checklist for My Family*, she has written *Checklist for Family Caregivers*, a guide to help you managing your responsibilities as a caregiver. For those who have lost a family member, *Checklist for Family Survivors* helps you get through all the practical and legal matters you need to handle. *Wise Moves: Where to Live, What to Consider, and Whether to Stay or Go* helps you navigate all the things you need to consider in deciding whether you change where you live and sets out clearly the options available. *Get the Most Out of Retirement: Checklist for Happiness, Health, Purpose, and Financial Security* aims to help you prepare for the change of lifestyle and finances and inspire you to make the most of your years.

Hurme worked at AARP for 23 years, explaining tough issues in plain language, and is a nationally recognized elder law attorney.

She has written more than twenty law review articles on elder law topics and lectured on elder abuse and surrogate decision making in Australia, Czech Republic, Germany, Great Britain, Italy, Japan, Korea, Moldova, the Netherlands, Scotland, and Spain. In 2010, she delivered an Honor Lecture at the World Congress on Adult Guardianship in Yokohama, Japan. She is also in demand as a speaker, having given over 100 presentations on elder law topics in at least 40 states. Hurme can be viewed talking about *Getting Your Legal Life in Order* as a Great Courses lecturer.

For the past two decades, her volunteer commitment has focused on the rights of adults with diminished capacity and the reform of guardianship policy and procedures. She has served multiple terms on the boards of the National Guardianship Association and the Center for Guardianship Certification, where she has been instrumental in developing standards for guardians and criteria to improve professional competency. Hurme is a past chair of the National Guardianship Network, a collaboration of 12 national organizations working to improve guardianship. She was an adviser to the Uniform Law Commission in the drafting of the Uniform Adult Guardianship and Protective Proceedings Jurisdiction Act, which has been quickly adopted in 44 states, the District of Columbia, and Puerto Rico. Hurme also participated in the drafting of the Uniform Guardianship, Conservatorship and Other Protective Proceedings Act, a major step in the reform of guardianship procedures. She was a member of U.S. State Department delegation to the Hague Conference on Private International

Law that drafted the International Convention on the Protection of Incapacitated Adults. In 2008, she was honored by the National College of Probate Judges with the William Treat Award for Excellence in probate law.

Hurme started her legal career as a partner in a private law firm, gained valuable experience serving older clients as a legal services attorney, and served as a magistrate in Alexandria, Virginia. She spent three years as an attorney adviser with the U.S. Department of Justice Office of Intelligence Policy and Review. She then returned to elder law advocacy as an assistant staff attorney with the American Bar Association Commission on Law and Aging before moving to AARP. Hurme taught elder law as an adjunct professor at the George Washington University Law School for eight years, honing her ability to explain the law. She is a long-term member of the National Academy of Elder Law Attorneys and the Virginia and District of Columbia bars. Hurme served as a member of the Discipline and Ethics Commission of the Certified Financial Planners Board of Standards.

She received her B.A. from Newcomb College of Tulane University, New Orleans, Louisiana, and received her J.D. *cum laude* from the Washington College of Law, American University, Washington, D.C. She lives in Bridgewater, Virginia, where she is a full-time caregiver for her husband while continuing to write books, garden, kayak, and enjoy time with her grandchildren.